Penguin Books

Toddler Tactics

Pinky McKay is a Melbourne-based writer and editor specialising in health, education and family issues. An International Board Certified Lactation Consultant (IBCLC) and certified infant massage instructor, Pinky is the author of *Sleeping Like a Baby*, *Parenting By Heart* and *100 Ways to Calm the Crying*. She writes two monthly columns for *Practical Parenting Magazine* and contributes to various national and international publications and websites including *Littlies* magazine (New Zealand), Kindred, Bellybelly, Bubhub, Motherinc and Kidslife.

The mother of four adult 'children' and a now-teenage 'bonus baby' (the baby you have when your other kids can run their own baths, tie their own shoelaces and even drive their own cars), Pinky's greatest pleasure is enjoying the precious giggles of her two delightful grandchildren – one of whom is a terrific toddler!

By the same author:

Parenting by Heart
100 Ways to Calm the Crying
Sleeping Like a Baby

Toddler Tactics

PINKY McKAY

Penguin Books

PENGUIN BOOKS

Published by the Penguin Group
Penguin Group (Australia)
707 Collins Street, Melbourne, Victoria 3008, Australia
(a division of Penguin Australia Pty Ltd)
Penguin Group (USA) Inc.
375 Hudson Street, New York, New York 10014, USA
Penguin Group (Canada)
90 Eglinton Avenue East, Suite 700, Toronto, Canada ON M4P 2Y3
(a division of Pearson Penguin Canada Inc.)
Penguin Books Ltd
80 Strand, London WC2R 0RL England
Penguin Ireland
25 St Stephen's Green, Dublin 2, Ireland
(a division of Penguin Books Ltd)
Penguin Books India Pvt Ltd
11 Community Centre, Panchsheel Park, New Delhi – 110 017, India
Penguin Group (NZ)
67 Apollo Drive, Rosedale, Auckland 0632, New Zealand
(a division of Pearson New Zealand Ltd)
Penguin Books (South Africa) (Pty) Ltd
Rosebank Office Park, Block D, 181 Jan Smuts Avenue, Parktown North,
Johannesburg 2196, South Africa
Penguin (Beijing) Ltd
7F, Tower B, Jiaming Center, 27 East Third Ring Road North,
Chaoyang District, Beijing 100020, China

Penguin Books Ltd, Registered Offices: 80 Strand, London, WC2R 0RL, England

First published by Penguin Group (Australia), 2008

5 7 9 10 8 6 4

Text copyright © Pinky McKay 2008

The moral right of the author has been asserted

Cover and text design by Karen Trump © Penguin Group (Australia)
Cover photograph by Veer
Typeset in 10/16 New Aster by Post Pre-press Group, Brisbane, Queensland
Printed and bound in Australia by McPherson's Printing Group,
Maryborough, Victoria

National Library of Australia
Cataloguing-in-Publication data:

McKay, Pinky, 1952–.
Toddler tactics.
Includes index.
ISBN 978 0 14 300581 0 (pbk.).
1. Toddlers – Care – Handbooks, manuals, etc. 2. Toddlers – Development –
Handbooks, manuals, etc. 3. Toddlers – Psychological aspects – Handbooks,
manuals, etc. 4. Child rearing. 5. Parenting. I. Title.

649.122

penguin.com.au

Contents

A note from the author   vi

Introduction   1

1 How does your toddler grow?   5

2 Look who's talking   33

3 Moving and grooving   49

4 Behave yourself!   59

5 Play and learning   116

6 Routines and rituals   157

7 Let's eat   175

8 Toilet training   208

9 Caring for teeth, skin and hair   222

10 Goodnight, sleep tight   230

11 Another baby   260

12 Becoming independent   275

13 Love, laugh, enjoy   296

Resources   298

Further reading   307

Acknowledgements   309

Index   312

A note from the author

Because children come in both genders, I have alternated the terms 'he' and 'she' throughout this book – no sexism intended. Boys and girls have equal ability to challenge and delight their parents.

Introduction

Do you:

- ❀ Automatically tie your shoelaces in double knots?
- ❀ Ever pour your coffee into a sippy cup?
- ❀ Cover your fridge with neo-preschooler art?
- ❀ Point out horsies and moo-cows when you go for a drive – any drive, anywhere, regardless of who is in the car with you?
- ❀ Collect empty cereal boxes and margarine containers?
- ❀ Appreciate dandelions without stems as much as long-stemmed roses?
- ❀ Snap to attention whenever you hear a child cry, 'Mummy!'?
- ❀ Know that adults can function on a lot less than eight hours' sleep?
- ❀ Feel absolutely certain your child is the most wonderful, fascinating, unique little person in the entire universe (at least, most of the time)?

If you answered yes to two or more of these questions, *Toddler Tactics* is for you. Being the parent of a toddler can be exciting, exhilarating and exhausting – all at once! Your biddable baby has now become a moving, grooving tot with attitude, and all the changes that this entails can be confusing to you and your child. You are faced with issues such as discipline (what happens when your child discovers that 'no' is the most powerful word in his vocabulary?), eating (does tomato sauce count as a vegetable?), learning, teaching social skills, and trying to get enough sleep to keep up with your little dynamo.

Words such as hurry and tidy are meaningless to a toddler, yet we live in a fast-paced world that demands so much from us that frustration can be the order of most days: we are bombarded by pressure to be perfect parents – to have a well-behaved child who will comply as we race him from one educational activity to another lest he fail to achieve his academic potential when he reaches school age. When our tasks mount, it can be very tempting to simply pop on a DVD, especially if the manufacturers claim it will make your child smarter. But then taking the easy way (read, plonking him in front of the small screen) is sure to stir up guilty feelings that you may be letting your child down if you aren't an all-dancing, all-gluing entertainment coordinator.

Relax! *Toddler Tactics* will help you banish your performance anxiety and find the 'terrific' in your toddler.

Toddler Tactics offers a simple, fuss-free approach to enjoying and enhancing this magical stage of development. As the name suggests, *Toddler Tactics* is packed with practical strategies that you can use *right now* to overcome the inevitable challenges of living with a little person who is discovering the world and how it revolves around him (or not). I'll show how you can unleash your child's natural potential to be happy, bright and sociable without too many tears and tantrums (for you or your child!).

As well as offering practical strategies to encourage optimal development and cooperation without thwarting your child's innate spirit and sense of discovery, *Toddler Tactics* encourages you to be kind to yourself as you share this amazing journey with your child. Most importantly, remember to laugh lots – after all, it is very difficult to yell and laugh at the same time. And on some days (like when your child 'helps' by painting the new car/bathroom/cat/neighbour's child), if you don't laugh, you may well feel like crying!

Chapter one
How does your toddler grow?

Those sweet months of snuggling your tiny helpless baby in your arms went in a flash didn't they? And now you have a toddling tot who is growing and learning at breakneck speed. He will soon be able to walk and talk and feed himself; to learn what he is allowed to do (by pushing all the boundaries); to concentrate (watch him focus as he fiddles with every knob that is attached to an electric outlet, but please protect him with safety covers and switches); to climb (on tables, trees or the car roof!) and jump (off whatever he has climbed); and to share (after he learns the magic word 'mine!'). In just a few short years he will be asking questions that will have you on your toes as you struggle to explain why fish don't drown and where the sun goes at night.

'I could never have believed that having a son would be so rewarding. Not in a measurable sense, like a new car, but really emotionally and spiritually rewarding. We have grown together so much in just a year.

'I am in constant awe at his intuitiveness and ability to adapt to his surroundings. When he feels the need to point and show me everything he finds exciting I am spirited back to when I was a child and everything was new and untainted.'

Phil

For your child to reach this exciting stage of awareness, an enormous amount of development takes place during the baby and toddler years. Scientists tell us that approximately half of a child's intelligence is developed by the age of four. This means that your child will learn faster in the first four years than in the next forty.

The role of being first teacher to your little dynamo might seem like an awesome responsibility and it is, but it can be loads of fun and it isn't too difficult. If you become involved and tune in to your little wonder, you will naturally provide enough love and stimulating experiences to enable your child to reach his potential. Just think, as he interacts with you every day, your tot will learn music ('here we go round the mulberry bush'), maths (one peg, two pegs), science (where does the moon go?), art (finger painting and playdough), human relations (your turn, my turn) and language skills (I love you).

If you are feeling a little overawed at the pressure of

being in charge of your child's academic future, please relax. Your little one's innate hunger to learn will mean that he will create ample opportunities to satisfy his own rapidly growing intellect – from smearing bum cream on the cat to tipping your perfume down the loo. Seriously though, there are lots of resources to help you skill up so that you can stay one step ahead of your very clever kid. In particular, see the Raising Children Network website listed in the Resources section at the back of this book.

Every toddler develops at a different rate and, although it is possible to enhance a child's developmental potential, it is unwise to force the natural sequence of development, particularly through inappropriate use of commercial equipment. For instance, infants who are propped into baby walkers and walk without learning to crawl first may appear awfully clever right now compared to their creeping peers, but may experience difficulty learning to read and write because important brain connections haven't been developed by the activity of crawling. (See Moving and grooving, page 48.)

Just as with physical growth, there will be spurts of intellectual development and at times it may seem that progress in one area is proceeding at the expense of others. For instance, speech development may take second place to the mastery of walking, climbing and other physical skills (or vice versa), but if you observe your child carefully and give him appropriate opportunities, he will develop just as nature intended.

Of course, if you feel concerned that your child is having difficulties in any area it is wise to seek an objective opinion. Be warned: you may have to navigate a veritable maze to find appropriate help. If the advice you receive seems inappropriate, or if you feel undermined or are still worried, seek another opinion and remind yourself you are not an overanxious parent taking up professionals' precious time – you are contributing to their kids' school fees! Above all, you are the expert about *your* child.

Wonderful ones

The label 'one-year-old' really is a broad generalisation. Any parent of an eighteen-month-old will affirm that their determined little being is worlds apart from the comparatively compliant twelve-month-old who was content to follow them from room to room, picking up and exploring objects, but also quite easily diverted from potential danger.

Even one-year-olds who are the same age can seem vastly different in development. Some just-turned one-year-olds may still be crawling on all fours, others will be cruising around furniture, and some may have been walking for a couple of months. Some just-ones have several teeth, others may be just starting to teethe. Some will be mostly pointing and grunting, while others may already say quite a few words. Often children will make headway in physical development, then start to talk or vice versa – a baby who is less physical may be more of a talker. Eventually, they will all even-out with language and physical skills.

'Everything is a delight to twelve-month-old Griffin. He isn't walking alone yet (he cruises around furniture and from one object to another as long as he is touching the next "base", and when he is in a hurry he crawls really fast!), but he has a large vocabulary and talks non-stop. He is starting to join some words together like "nanny, car, broom" – he loves going out in Nana's car – and "cow moo". He points and throws himself to what he wants saying, "This! this! this!" He is fascinated with the autumn leaves and makes me take him outside to look at the "trees". His favourite game is cooking, and he likes to empty the pots and Tupperware out of the cupboard and stir them with a wooden spoon.

'Griffin likes to throw things on the floor and then holds his hands palm-up to show they're empty. He thinks this is hilarious, and after he throws an object he points and makes you

*pick it up and give it to him so he can throw it again and again
if you are silly enough to keep playing his game.*

   *'He is obsessed with buttons and, at his insistence, I
hold him up to press light switches, buttons on the washing
machine, dryer and microwave. He opens and shuts the CD
player, DVD player and Xbox and puts discs in and out and
opens and closes them. This is not something we encourage
but he has taught himself.'*

Larissa

By the second half of the first year, physiological changes
occurring in her brain are responsible for an expansion of
your toddler's moods as well as playing, talking, thinking
and socialising skills. Although it is wonderfully exciting
to watch your little dynamo running and climbing as she
explores her environment with enthusiasm and chatters
with new words every day, her behavioural changes can
become challenging: your tot will have a will of her own,
and her sudden grasp of language at about eighteen to
twenty months (experts refer to this vocabulary spurt as
the 'naming explosion') will not only enable her to communicate more effectively but also insistently!

Although your eighteen-month-old will absorb information like a tiny sponge, she won't yet have developed

the ability to fully process it all and will often be over-whelmed. For instance, her apparent defiance when you ask for her cooperation is really due to a lack of under-standing. Although she may 'parrot' your warnings, she will return to climbing up on the stool or poking at the electrical socket, so be prepared to repeat yourself (as well as childproof your environment) and physically move her (over and over again) to protect her from potential hazards. When we consider that the nerves that *produce* emotions mature before those that *control* them, it is easier to under-stand the reasons behind meltdowns when you do thwart an 'adventure'.

On the upside, you will now have a better idea what your toddler is telling you as she points and exclaims with delight. It really is a fascinating experience to know what your little child is thinking and to share a wonder-filled world through her eyes.

'My daughter Savannah is eighteen months old. A hilarious, divine, smiley, wide-eyed, Rubenesque toddler. I worked as a nanny for a number of years and thought I knew everything there was to know about babies. What a shock it was to find I knew everything about other babies but absolutely nothing about my own. I thought I would love being the mother of an *infant. I was wrong. I thought being the mother of a toddler would drive me insane. I was wrong again.*

'Every day I spend with Savannah I laugh, sometimes until I cry. Every day we make what used to be a mundane chore into a wild adventure (today we washed the garage doors!). Every day we share impromptu kisses and cuddles.

'Every day I spend too many minutes staring at my daughter in wonder. How can she sit for an hour trying to put her shoes on and not get frustrated because the buckles are still done up? How could she prove every naysayer wrong by happily joining us driving from Brisbane to Perth, and back? How can she climb into bed with me in the mornings for a breastfeed, be so big and grown up and still be my tiny baby?

'For every minute of my daughter's babyhood that was difficult, depressing or frustrating, the hours of laughter and joy have repaid them a million times over.'

Elizabeth

'I love the cuddlyness of my twenty-month-old son right now. I love how he is exploring the world but I am his default and my lap is his "base" to return to, his security when he's scared and his source of comfort when he's upset and struggling to deal with all the new emotions that he's experiencing. I love watching him grow and mentally expand his horizons. I love *how tender he is with other children and how he hugs all of his friends before he says goodbye.'*

Sonia

Toddler tactic: create a safe space

One-year-olds are intrepid adventurers but they have little sense of danger. This means that protective eyes (yours!) are needed to oversee them at every waking moment. To take a break from this intensive parenting, create a safe, contained space by childproofing a room such as your toddler's bedroom or playroom so that there is nothing to fall off and no small pieces to choke on or poke into body holes. If you provide some interesting toys and use a door barrier, you can snatch a few minutes peace to have a shower or do some chores while your child safely amuses himself.

Terrific twos

She can do cute and she can do sweet but what your two-year-old does really well is attitude! Think stomping feet and an emphatic *no!* And, of course, the sideways glance first to check that you are actually taking notice before she performs her daring acts of defiance. Your just-turned two-year-old will swing from loving and affectionate to out of control; she will venture forth independently one minute and cling to you the next; and her favourite saying could be 'me do it'. Although her clinginess may be frustrating to you, it is best to meet your little one's needs for security without a fuss. This way, her confidence will increase and she will gradually take bigger 'steps' because she knows there is a safe base where she can return and refuel her 'confidence tank' when the world seems overwhelming.

Even if you have to dig deep to find the terrific in your toddler some days, she will be nice far more often than she is 'naughty' (honestly!) and she really can't help being emotional: according to the experts, her volatile temperament is not naughtiness, but due to her emerging sense of independence and self-discovery as she learns to assert her personality. This doesn't mean you have to allow your little rascal to run you ragged as she tests every boundary, but do be patient and try to pick your battles and, just occasionally, let her win a few. (See Teaching good behaviour, page 72.)

'I just love the fact that my little boy absolutely adores me, no matter if I have had a grumpy mummy day or a great mummy day. He melts me with his smile; he makes me so proud with his enthusiasm for life and his sensitivity towards my feelings.

I love his kisses, the way he idolises his big sister, and the deep and meaningful moments we have. I tell him I love him very much, then he tells me, "I love you too, Mummy. Happy birthday, Mummy." It's so hard not to giggle at his beautiful sentiments!'

Kelly

There are huge leaps in motor development and language in the second year and, at about two and a half, connections between the left and right hemispheres of the brain enable children to use both sides of their bodies independently. This means that, instead of finding it difficult to use each hand without the other mirroring its action, toddlers will soon be able to complete a task such as holding a banana in one hand as they peel it with the other or hold a cup steady while they pour water into it with the other hand. By almost three, your child may even be able to manage cutting with scissors as he holds the paper steady with his other hand.

Your two-year-old will not only run and climb with increasing agility and balance but he will begin to jump, and at almost three he may even hop on one foot. He will be able to catch a balloon, then a ball and, with practice, he might be able to kick a moving ball. He will learn his colours, at first matching two objects the same colour, then he will name colours and choose coloured clothing or objects as requested. Painting is a great activity to stimulate colour awareness (see Creative play, page 141), while playing finger games and modelling with playdough and clay will help hone fine motor skills as it develops your toddler's hand muscles. Perhaps the biggest milestone after the age of two is leaving the world of nappies behind (at least during the day), but, like any important milestone, the timing of this depends on your child's physiological readiness so please don't push. See chapter 8 for more on toilet training.

As your child becomes more verbally expressive and physically capable, her frustrations will gradually disappear and life will become calmer. Meanwhile, enjoy your two-year-old's spunky spirit and remember the mummy mantra: 'This too shall pass'. I promise it will – all too soon!

Toddler tactic: make play safe

Your two-year-old is likely to be very active as he learns about his body and how it moves in space. As well as providing plenty of outdoor play opportunities such as swimming, running in the park, climbing and ball play, make a place where active play is allowed inside – a mattress on the floor for jumping, space for dancing or an obstacle course of pillows and large empty boxes or upturned chairs to climb through.

To reduce car seat battles with your little wriggler, take his car seat inside and let him play at strapping his toys in. Show your child what 'safe' means by showing him what happens when teddy is in the seat and falls over without his belt on. In the car, make sure your toddler is comfortable and has toys that are within reach, or play games (red light, stop! Green light, go! Or, 'can you see a yellow car?') and sing together. A harmonica is a wonderful diversion – he won't be able to make 'music' and yell at the same time!

Thrilling threes

Your three-year-old is full of wonder – everything is magical as his days are busily spent exploring, observing and imitating. Who, what, where and why questions are the order of the day. Yet, despite the magic and wonder, there is a touch of the dark side to the three-year-old, at least that's what it can seem like after the terrific twos. After all, they were reputed to be terrible and you survived them fairly easily in comparison to the threes.

When a little friend's mother asks, 'Does your child always behave like this?' you feel your anxiety levels rising. Behave like what, you wonder? Thankfully, your three-year-old is an angel when he is out, despite being rather a rascal at home. It so happens that he not only behaves nicely when visiting, he gets a sticker for diligently helping tidy up at preschool, but at home when you ask for help to pack away his toys he growls, 'Go away.' And that's not all. His language is likely to extend to phrases like, 'It's not fair,' and even 'I hate you!' This 'no more Mr Nice Baby' attitude has you wondering whether you are rearing a three-year-old or an adolescent in small clothes.

According to developmental psychologist Jean Piaget, your 'threenager's' behaviour is a sign of advancing development, what he calls the 'preoperational period'. This is when children perceive themselves as kings of the universe, so when you tell your toddler to put on a jacket because it's raining and he says, 'But I won't get wet,' he isn't being defiant, he actually believes in his own omnipotence. Although it can be hard to bear (and makes you wonder where you went wrong), your three-year-old is struggling to move between infancy into early childhood, and a lot of rewiring is happening in his little brain. He is struggling with control and his new grasp of language allows him to inflict pain.

The best way to deal with this is to treat it as a game, albeit one that you will want to discourage: try to stay calm and don't take your child's behaviour personally. There is no point in going head to head with a person who thinks he is king of the world! Instead, let your little one have increasing control over the things that don't really matter. She needs to clean her teeth and wear a seat belt but it doesn't matter if she wants to wear gumboots with her best dress.

Of course, there are a lot of thrilling things about your three-year-old's development, especially his language skills. Although he doesn't yet understand 'yesterday' and 'tomorrow' in an adult sense, he understands 'now', 'soon' and 'later'; he can listen attentively to short books and will enjoy familiar stories (heaven help you if you change the words or skip a page!); he can repeat simple rhymes and carry a tune as he sings little songs and he will be able to 'read' his own stories from picture books.

Your three-year-old will be interested in perfecting her advancing motor skills – she may spend an entire morning going down a slide or riding her trike. She will now be able to stand, balance and hop on one foot, she can catch a large ball, and throw and kick a ball forward. If your toddler finds it easy to kick a stationary ball, introduce a running kick and then a drop kick.

Perhaps the most thrilling thing about your three-year-old is that he really is becoming an independent person. He will soon be out of nappies and managing to take himself to the loo without help (except to make sure his bottom is clean), as well as washing his hands and cleaning his teeth (with supervision). Your 'big' toddler will be able to dress himself and put his own shoes on (but laces are still too tricky to manage), and he will be able to feed himself with a spoon and small fork. Do encourage and praise every effort – and be ready to help him on days when he doesn't feel so big.

'When our first child turned three it was such a magical time. Responding to the questions of an intensely curious toddler helped me to look at life from a different perspective. It helped me appreciate the beauty and simplicity of things around me, rather than being swept up in the analytical, fast-paced adult world. To step out of the frantic pace of modern city living and indulge in the magical world of a toddler is such a sweet and liberating thing to do.'

Alice

'Our big bouncing lad Finn has just turned three, and is reminding me so much of a Labrador pup. He is full of energy and is

interested in everything in the world. As much as he likes sniffing out mischief, he's really enjoying the fact he can easily find his own jacket, boots and hat, and head outside with a quick, "See you later, Mumma," over his shoulder. He can remember the words to his favourite songs, and the role-playing he does with his toy people, cars and trains shows that a colourful imagination is alive and well in his gorgeous head. He's fascinated with insects of all sorts, and how trains move on tracks, and how the day changed to night. He wants to know everything. He asks us why at least thirty times a day. He finds something good in most things he comes across. I love that aspect of this age. Negativity isn't very common (unless it's time to get out of the bath and he doesn't want to). Now that his communication is at a stage where we don't struggle to understand him, he is just much more relaxed than he was when two, as he doesn't need to work at explaining something or pointing. The words simply spill out (and often).

'He delights in his friends and small pleasures, such as a walk in the park with the dog. I can have him clapping with glee by simply suggesting we go watch a train pull into the station. I love that he appreciates me, and thanks me often for little things which I have not realised were so important. He makes me aware daily how important.'

Donna

Toddler tactic: handling questions

'Why' is a very good word – it helps children make sense of things they don't understand if their questions are answered simply. It can also get your attention. Not only will your three-year-old ask endless questions but she will often repeat what she has told you, over and over. One way to prevent too much repetition and to help her thinking skills is to show her you really are listening. When she asks, 'Where does the sun go at night?' reflect her question back to her as, 'Where do you think the sun goes at night?' If she tells you what she thinks, reflect her answer back to her, 'Oh, the sun hides behind the trees.' If she responds by asking why, reflect her question again and ask her, 'Why does the sun hide behind the trees?'

Even if it is quite nerve-wracking, tell her that she asks very good questions. When you need a break from question time, your child is more likely to be respectful as you tell her, 'I am sorry I can't answer any more questions until after lunch. I have to put the baby to bed/make a phone call/cook dinner (whatever), so perhaps you could play with your blocks or help me chop the beans (create a diversion).'

You can also reflect back to your child when she repeats herself endlessly. This way she will feel heard and with luck she will either extend her conversation (which encourages language development) or wander off happy that she has been acknowledged.

Personality plus

Just as his fingerprints are his alone, your child's personality is unique. As parents we wonder, can we take all the credit (or blame) for our child's temperament? Could he be a 'chip off the old block' or is it the fantastic environment we have provided that makes our child so easy-going? Or have we inadvertently caused our child to be 'supersensitive' or too 'dependent'?

> *'My daughter was being a total drama queen one day. I turned to my friend and sighed, "Where did I get her from?" My friend quickly sorted me out, replying, "She's just like her mother!"'*
>
> **Trish**

Your child's temperament may be a neat fit with your own, or not. You may be a 'bookish' person who imagined reading endlessly to your little one but find instead you are the parent of a jumping bean who never sits still. Or you may be an athlete who hoped to teach your tot the finer points of football as soon as he could stand but have a sensitive, cautious child who flinches whenever you throw a ball at him. You may wonder, 'Where did this child come from?' but it would be more enlightening to ask yourself what this little being has to teach you.

'I read to Jack in the womb and then three shiny picture books a day from birth and he couldn't care less about books. I blend up an array of fresh vegetables and he wants bread and potato chips. I vowed there would be no television, imagining we would spend the days feeding ducks and digging in the sand pit. He loves The Wiggles.'

Tania

Whether you can mould your child's temperament or whether he is born with a particular tendency to be easy-going and calm or serious and sensitive, a thoughtful leader or a daredevil, his personality will blossom with your acceptance of the unique individual that he is, and the loving encouragement that you give to his positive traits. It is up to you to channel and develop your child's special qualities. For instance, a sensitive child may need extra doses of reassurance and support to feel secure, an active child will need constructive outlets for his energy, and a quieter child may need encouragement to get involved.

It isn't a good idea to label your child, because whether it is 'good' or 'bad' your child's self-image will be affected by his label, and he will probably live up to it. It may be reassuring to note that characteristics parents find most challenging in toddlers can be highly regarded attributes later in life: when your 'wilful' toddler is six feet tall, people will be praising his 'drive', 'commitment' and 'perseverance'; people will admire your active toddler's 'energy' when she is a grown woman; and your sensitive child could become the most caring adult. In fact, try rethinking descriptions of your child right now. To appreciate the positives, see your little daydreamer as 'imaginative'; your noisy child as enthusiastic; your argumentative tot as independent; and your inattentive little soul as a global thinker with a wide focus! If you are at a loss for positive labels some days, 'unique' or 'motivated' are perfectly acceptable as long as they are meant with appreciation and love.

Influencing factors

It is so much fun to watch your child reveal his unique personality. As well as his inborn characteristics, there are many outside influences that affect how this wee person will turn out as he grows. Some of these influences can be tempered, but others will be less under your control, especially as he is cared for by people outside your home environment (child care, school, etc.). These influences include:

❀ his place in the family
❀ the age gap between siblings
❀ gender.

Place in the family
Although each child's experience within a family will be unique, it seems that what our children miss out on the swings, they will catch up on the roundabouts of sibling placement. While first-borns receive more attention and adult guidance, it seems they also have more pressure. They may be high achievers but they could be more anxious than their younger siblings, who are likely to benefit from more experienced, relaxed parents.

Because every 'first' with your firstborn is new and exciting, and later there is a level of sentimentality around the baby of the family, middle children are sometimes resentful of the parental attention given to the other children. Middle children usually have to fight a little harder for their parents' attention and may crave the family spotlight. On a positive note, many middle children grow up more relaxed than their older siblings (who may feel pressure to achieve) and more responsible than their indulged younger brother or sister.

I personally believe that difficulties related to family

placement are closely related to our own attitudes and labelling. Stereotypes can generally be avoided by being aware of each child's individuality. Try to celebrate what you love about each of your children and remind yourself that love is like a great big chocolate cake – there's enough to share among everyone. Wherever they come in the family and however their relationship with you is influenced by this, you have an endless capacity to love them all uniquely.

Age gaps between siblings

When children are closely spaced, or if they are twins, it can be convenient for parents if they play together, dress alike, and share friends, toys and activities, but this may make it difficult to develop individuality, so try and give each child some 'one on one' time and observe what your little ones seem uniquely interested in.

Even though the differences between children are amazing to parents, please avoid comparing your children with each other (or anybody else) – there is nothing more dampening to a child's spirit than to be told, 'Your sister doesn't behave like this,' or 'Your brother is the clever one.'

Toddler tactic: help twins to become individuals

There is only one perfect child in the whole world and she is yours! That is, unless she is a twin. While parents of single children compare their lot favourably with other people's children, twins are usually compared with one another. Don't let anybody label either of your twins as the chubby one, the one who is talking, the clever one, the shy one or anything else because this can be a step on the slippery slope to fragile self-esteem or sibling rivalry.

Help twins develop their own identities:

❀ *Dress them differently.*

❀ *Refer to them by name, not as 'the twins'.*

❀ *Encourage each child to develop their own interests and skills, just as you would if they weren't twins.*

❀ *If one twin is behaving inappropriately, remove her and deal with her privately so they both don't feel 'bad'.*

❀ *Give separate presents at birthdays and have separate birthday cakes.*

❀ *Most importantly, find creative ways to spend time alone with each child.*

Gender

You may be able to keep your girl out of pink but it is more difficult to temper the media message that 'pink is only for girls'. Television doesn't always portray male and female role models as rigidly as 'The Brady Bunch' any more, but role models still include superheroes for boys and Barbies (and lots of pink!) for girls.

Research suggests there are some innate differences between boys and girls at an early age and these are thought to be due to brain structure: boys are generally thought to be better at activities controlled by the right side of the brain which may make them more physically competent, while early development in the left side of girls' brains seems to hone their fine motor skills. Generally, girls seem to be more socially adept and prefer to interact with people, and boys tend to be as interested in objects as they are in people. When it comes to language skills, it seems that girls are ahead of boys, and this may be due, in part, to a more acute sense of hearing. Language skills can also be reflected in the ways boys and girls play: girls' play is usually more word-based while boys' is more action-based, with both engaging in games that involve role play.

Although children develop gender awareness at about two, they don't really understand what this means or that girls and (especially) boys are expected to behave in a particular way. Although most people don't bat an eyelid at spunky little girls who wear overalls, there is often a deep level of anxiety and discomfort about little boys who want to dress up in boas and beads. Actually, this dressing-up phase is quite normal and, rather than causing any long-term damage to their psyche (as long as you don't overreact), it could have some surprising educational benefits. According to a report published by the UK Centre for Language in Primary Education entitled 'Boys and Reading', a little 'gender bending' could help to close the literacy gap between boys and girls. The report found that pursuing 'girly' imaginative play that centres on roles and relationships helps develop an important understanding of stories and can improve reading and language skills.

We could probably argue until the cows come home whether the differences between girls and boys are due to nature or nurture but does it matter? What matters are the messages you give children about what it means to be a girl or boy because these ideas are powerful and indelible. Whether your toddler is a boy who loves Barbies and frills and would talk the leg off an iron pot, or a girl who refuses to wear a dress and always has grubby knees, please delight in his or her uniqueness: both boys and girls need opportunities to enjoy being who they are and experimenting without pressure to conform to rigid gender roles.

Here are some ways to show your acceptance of your child regardless of their gender:

✿ Choose stories (or make some up) that show girls can be superheroes and boys can be domestic. For instance, when you tell 'The Three Bears', Mother Bear can mend the broken stool while Father Bear makes more porridge.

✿ Provide dress-up clothes in exciting colours and textures for boys and girls. Allow your boy to dress up in high heels if he wants to – it won't turn him into a 'sheila' any more than letting your daughter wear a fireman's hat will bend her gender.

✿ Teach boys *and* girls to build, dress dolls, throw and kick balls, sew and do the dishes.

✿ Dress your little girl in practical clothes as well as pretty ones – it is very difficult to climb and be physically active in flowing skirts and dresses.

✿ Encourage girls to take risks and give them the message 'You are capable' rather than 'You are pretty'. Having had a daughter after two boys, I was staggered to see how people send strong messages to little girls through gifts as well as language: girls tend to be swamped with pretty dresses while boys receive blocks, trucks and tool sets. But girls like trucks, too, and boys can enjoy playing with dolls and soft toys.

✿ Boys need just as many cuddles as girls. It's okay for boys to cry, too. In fact, due to high levels of testosterone, boys may be slightly more vulnerable to stress, so please don't belittle your boy or try to make him 'tough' if he is emotional. If you show him it's okay to care, one day he will reward you with caring hugs and thoughtful gestures.

✿ Be an example yourself, as a person who will tackle problems and have adventures without slotting into a strict gender stereotype. Show, too, that you are proud of being a man or a woman.

Chapter two
Look who's talking

We eagerly await the first words, then the sentences that let us enter the magical world of our toddler in a new and exciting way. The journey from babble to banter is closely linked to emotion and the development of relationships, which means that your input is hugely important to help him become an articulate speaker. Loving, joyful interaction and responsiveness to your child's efforts to talk make a world of difference. When your little one is speaking, stop, get on his level and make eye contact as you listen.

'I'm loving the conversations I have with three-year-old Euan. He's very vocal and tells me the most wonderful stories. When I am working, he often plays with his dinosaurs on the floor of the office. He has the most wonderful conversations going on between the various dinosaurs and it reassures me that I am doing a good job.'

Mandy

Your baby has been developing his conversation skills from birth, or even earlier if we count all the listening he was doing while he was still inside you, but now that he is a toddler his speech skills will come together at breakneck speed.

From about **twelve months**, your child will learn approximately two words a week – that is, an exciting fifty words or so by the time he is eighteen months old. If your child is being reared in a bilingual environment, the number of words may be split between both languages and, at first, your little one's wonderful version of words may be understandable only to you or close family members.

Between **eighteen and twenty-four months**, language skills will really start to take off: experts call this the 'naming explosion' because your toddler could learn ten or more new words each day as he begins to label things in his environment – cup, car, ball, bath and so on. And, if he is really a little chatterbox, he could learn a new word every ninety minutes!

At about **twenty-four months** (remember, all children develop at their own individual pace), your toddler will begin stringing words together. However, his sense of grammar will take a while longer to evolve: he may say things like, 'Me go,' and use the same name for anything that falls into the same general category (that is, all animals with four legs might be 'dog' and – oh dear! – any man could be 'daddy'). Grammar skills are related to maturity of an area of the brain that is dedicated to processing language and storing all the rules needed for stringing words together into meaningful sentences. When your little chatterbox is developmentally ready, and has had lots of exposure to language, he will begin telling you about his world, describing his feelings and embarrassing you out loud and proud as he 'parrots' everything he hears – so watch your own language!

If you have any concerns about your toddler's language development (for instance, if he isn't using real words by the age of eighteen months, is frustrated by not being able to talk, has difficulty understanding what you say, stutters or isn't trying to speak in sentences by two and a half) check with your child health nurse or seek advice from a speech pathologist. As with any aspect of development, there is a wide spectrum of what is 'normal' when it comes to language skills, but consulting a specialist trained to diagnose and work with children having difficulty communicating will either reassure you or support you to help your child. And the earlier you seek help, the better.

Toddler tactic: use your 'nice' voice

You have taken care of your toddler since he was a baby, meeting his needs responsively. Is it any wonder he thinks he can tell you to 'pick it up' when he drops his crayon or demands, 'Mummy, juice!' Your tot isn't deliberately being bossy. He just doesn't have the words to express his needs more pleasantly. Teach your toddler to use his 'nice voice' by gently reminding him and showing him what you would like to hear. When he is closer to three you can be more explicit and tell him, 'My ears like to hear your nice voice and words like, "Mummy, please open the playdough. It's stuck."' You could even joke and say, "Mummy darling, pretty please, can you open the playdough?"

You can encourage a nice voice – and less bossiness and whining – by responding quickly when you hear your tot's nice voice. If you are busy or the request is inappropriate (such as a cake before dinner), you could say, 'I really like how you asked for cake. We can't have some right now because it's almost dinnertime, but we can have some after your bath.' Then make sure you do!

Also, take care to model your own nice voice, rather than giving your child orders such as, 'Get in the car,' or 'Pick up your toys, right now!'

To encourage your little chatterbox:

✿ **Name everything.** ' Doorknob', 'chair', 'dog', 'light'. Later, add adjectives to describe his favourite toys, people and objects: 'red jumper', 'cold milk', 'big truck'.

✿ **Listen.** Your child's attempts to use language will be reinforced when you pay attention, so remove background distractions such as the television and computer, and give your child your full attention. Get down to her level and make eye contact as you talk to her, then pause and listen as she takes a turn at responding.

✿ **Be a role model.** Talk to your child in clear, simple, relevant language, avoiding baby talk. Model language by using 'parallel talk'. This means talking about everything your child is doing while she is doing it. For example, while your child is scooting along on her ride-on, you could say, 'You are riding your train. Wow! You are pushing with your feet. I like the way you are riding your train.' When you're walking down the street, babble on about trees, cars, people, puddles – whatever your child sees, hears or smells. You can also model language by using 'self-talk', that is, talking about what *you* are doing as you work at home ('I am getting the milk out of the fridge and now I will make a cup of tea') or as you drive the car ('We are going round the corner at the traffic lights and we will buy some apples at the shop. Look at the big digger pushing the dirt into a hill!').

✿ **Support, don't criticise.** If somebody corrects you when you are doing your best, it doesn't inspire you to do better, does it? In fact, it might put you off trying for a while. So please don't correct your child when she makes an attempt to talk but gets it a little wrong. Instead of telling her, 'It is dog, not gog,' simply model the correct word without a fuss, 'Yes, a big black dog.'

✿ **Extend your child's vocabulary.** Your toddler's level of understanding will be ahead of his ability to express himself. As he attempts to talk, model advanced grammar, add information and extend your tot's vocabulary by repeating his words clearly and adding to them. For instance, if he says, 'Drink' (or 'dink') as he points animatedly at the fridge, you can say, 'You want a drink? Mummy will get you a drink.'

✿ **Extend language through experience.** Your toddler will learn more from seeing animals at the zoo or a farm than being shown flashcards. You can then enjoy a shared experience and expand his language skills by reading books about the animals he has seen, or take photos and make your own picture book. As you read about animals, create discussion: 'That's a big pink pig. He likes to roll in mud. What noise does the pig make?' Letting him help with household chores will create opportunities to talk, too. For instance, cooking together is a great hands-on experience that will extend your tot's vocabulary as you name ingredients, pour, chop and stir.

✿ **Exaggerate speech sounds.** Your child may acquire speech sounds much earlier or later than others, depending on coordination of the lips, tongue and palate. As your child matures, he will gradually correct his speech sound patterns. To encourage correct sounds, exaggerate them in words and play games with silly sounds. If silliness doesn't come easily, read Dr Seuss books for inspiration: 'He can go like a train, *choo, choo, choo, choo*. He can go like a clock. He can *tick*. He can *tock*.'

✿ **Be animated!** Shed those inhibitions by using gestures as you stress prepositions to help your tot understand 'behind', 'on top' and 'under'!

✿ **Sing along.** Whatever your singing ability, ban performance anxiety and sing with your child. Singing helps break words into syllables and slows down the sounds of speech. Consider, too, the repetition as little ones hear the words to familiar songs over and over. And, let's face it, since you are going to repeat yourself endlessly, it is far more fun to sing than to nag ('This is the way we pick up the toys').

Singing songs, chanting rhymes and playing a variety of music styles will also help develop memory and listening skills as well as the development of concepts such as high, low, over, under, up, down, big, small, shapes, numbers and so on. Singing is a fabulous way to encourage cooperation by establishing rhythm in your daily patterns and helping your little one's transition from one activity to another (bath time, bedtime, working songs, going in the car songs).

As well as singing, encourage language skills by using instruments (homemade or bought) to tell stories – do you remember *Peter and the Wolf*?

❧ **Read.** Read aloud every day, several times a day. Short books with rhyme and repetition will encourage your child to join in and 'read' with you. You can play games by waiting for him to finish the line of a favourite rhyming book. As you enjoy reading together, your poppet will be naturally, joyously extending his vocabulary and his feeling for word patterns that make up speech and grammar.

Encourage social language. You are your child's most powerful model as you help her develop social skills such as greeting people politely, taking turns in conversation, making eye contact while talking, and encouraging manners with words such as please, thank you and excuse me.

Toddler tactic: mind your language

Just as your child will copy your 'good' language, you can be sure she will repeat the 'bad' words she hears. Although it shouldn't come as a surprise, you may be stunned by just how precisely your cherub mimics your emotion the first time she shouts, 'Bloody idiot!' (or worse!). Naturally, you can bet your boots she will do this in a public place. So, apart from practising tactics such as pretending you are the babysitter: 'Mummy would be so sad to hear you talking like that', it is best to curb your own language and teach your little one some acceptable words to use for expressing emotions. 'Darn' or 'blast' mightn't cut it for you when you are really mad, but with a bit of practice and mindfulness, you will be able to keep your child's (and your own) language 'nice'. If your tot does swear, you can simply say, 'We don't say bad words.' If she insists, 'But you do!', you might reply, 'Well, if you promise not to say bad words, I won't either.'

'When Elijah was about eighteen months old, he got the word "truck" mixed up with something you don't really want to hear! I was shocked, my firstborn thought it was funny, and my brothers and sister (all younger than me and without kids) thought it was hilarious. I don't think I dealt with it particularly well. It was embarrassing when he'd shout out in public, "Mummy, look, a f***." I did feel a bit better when I heard from other mothers that their sons did the same at that age. But he grew out of it. I think the best thing is to play it down and ignore as best you can, without bringing attention to it. I would just reply, "Yes, a truck," emphasising the "t"!'

Kelly

Sign language

Knowing exactly what you want but being unable to convey this except through a grunt accompanied by desperate gestures must be very frustrating. Perhaps this is why baby signing is becoming the new buzzword among parents of relatively inarticulate toddlers.

Although you can start signing to babies from a few weeks old, most parents start signing between six and twelve months when infants can respond by signing back. With lots of repetition, toddlers will quickly start indicating their needs in simple gestures to represent words that are meaningful to them such as 'more', 'milk', 'bath', 'bed', 'ball'.

Long before your little one begins to talk, he will start to express himself through gestures such as waving goodbye, clapping hands and blowing kisses. Teaching your tot specific signs to express his needs and wants is simply an extension of baby body language. The theory behind baby signing is that infants' hand and body coordination develops more quickly than the coordination of oral development required for clear speech.

Just as with oral language, at first your toddler will understand the signs you make to him before he is able to make signs back to you, but with a bit of practice you will come to understand one another. Although some parents worry that signing may delay speech, proponents of infant signing say the opposite is true – baby signing can actually extend your child's vocabulary. There is even evidence that signing can raise a child's IQ by improving communication and stimulating intellectual development.

Signing, say the experts, is about enhancing language, not replacing it, so they advise using signs with normal speech. This means that as you sign to your child, you also say the word so your little one makes the link between gesture and word.

One of the most important differences between spoken and sign language is the eye contact involved: because your baby is looking at you, she's concentrating hard on what you're saying as well as what you're doing. According to Jo Kennedy, director of the Australian baby signing program Fingers and Thumbs, there are lasting benefits in learning the skill of making and maintaining eye contact, including enhanced parent–child bonding and a sense of security; increased confidence; heightened empathy and social skills as children are encouraged to read body language. From a neurological perspective, signing stimulates the language and visual receptors of the brain, which in turn will be reinforced by the physical act of signing.

When your baby can sign back (which requires close observation from you), communication becomes two-way. If, for example, she tells you she can hear a plane, you can respond, 'You heard a plane? Yes, I can see it up in the sky. Isn't it loud?' In this way, you are spending focused time talking to your child, which is one of the best ways of helping speech develop.

'People often comment that my children are very engaging. We figured out it's because they demand eye contact when talking. They also place themselves in front of us or tap our

upper arm to achieve eye contact. Only then will they proceed with their all-important story while holding our gaze.

'At the dinner table we ritually share stories about our day. Even our three-year-old will demand, "It's my turn. You're not listening. Look at me." This has come about incidentally. I have taught sign language to all my children from when they were babies (I worked with children who were deaf for many years) but I didn't realise that the habit of maintaining eye contact was such a powerful skill for hearing children. It has helped them when making new friends as they have not been afraid to look someone in the eye.

'My husband, however, dreads sitting down to read the paper at the kitchen table with me. As we speak, I constantly expect him to look at me to show me he is listening!'

Jo Kennedy, director, Fingers and Thumbs

How to start signing

⚜ **Make it fun!** Just as you introduce any new skill to your little one, it's important to go at your tot's pace and remember that children learn most when they are enjoying themselves. If you take the approach that signing is another positive way to engage with your child, rather than a task to make her smarter, it will be a stress-free game and learning will happen naturally.

❀ **Tune in to your child's interests.** Little ones quickly pick up the sign for 'more' in relation to food!

❀ **Use words, too.** Whenever you show your child a sign, say the word as well. Always use the same sign, repeat it often, and emphasise the word along with the sign, so your baby can clearly see and hear the connection: 'Do you want some more? You'd like some more, would you? Okay, let's get you some more!'

❀ **Be patient.** Your tot may try signing to you after a few days or it may take several weeks. Keep watching and making eye contact as you sign and talk to your child, and you will both be having fun, whatever else happens.

To find out more about signing see under 'Parenting information and support' in the Resources section at the back of this book.

Teaching more than one language

During his first year of life, your baby's brain was being 'wired' for sound recognition. By the time he was six months old, he would have developed tonal memories to whatever languages he was exposed to and this exposure will make it easier for him to learn multiple languages later in life. Neuropsychologist Dr Patricia Kuhl of the University of Washington in Seattle explains that newborns can learn any sound in any language and can distinguish all of the different sounds that humans speak. By six months of age, babies already have different auditory maps, depending on the language they have been exposed to. By twelve months, infants have lost the ability to discriminate sounds that are not significant in their language and their babbling has acquired the sounds of their native language.

Research also confirms that learning multiple languages is easier for little children than adults. Using magnetic resonance imaging techniques to map brain activity in healthy adults, researchers at Sloan Kettering Cancer Centre in New York found that adults who had learned two languages as very young children stored both languages together in the same area of the brain. Those who acquired a second language in adolescence used a separate region of the brain.

This research suggests that while babies and toddlers appear to learn the languages in their environment relatively easily, and that their brain encodes these languages into hard-wired neuronal circuits, adolescents and adults must use a different – and more difficult – process to learn and retain the information.

If two languages are spoken in your home or family (for example, by grandparents), experts suggest that the best approach is 'one person, one language'. For instance, if one carer uses the second language exclusively, this will help your child separate and learn both languages more easily than exposing him to two languages from one carer.

If you are not a native speaker, but would like to introduce your toddler to another language, it is important to expose him to people who are. You might consider taking your child to a bilingual playgroup or preschool and also use tapes of songs, storybooks and DVDs to enhance your child's experience. Or, you could hire a babysitter or nanny who speaks another language. Remember to stick to the one-person, one-language rule.

Most importantly, praise your child for speaking his second language and relax about the finer details of grammar and sentence structure. Exposure and enjoyment are the keys to fostering a positive attitude towards a rich language experience.

Chapter three
Moving and grooving

Your toddler's amazing intellectual growth isn't isolated from other aspects of development. It is dependent on sensory and motor skills which help increase her understanding of the world. For instance, the 'cross-patterning' movement (using the opposite arm and leg together) required for crawling aids the development of pathways that connect the left and right hemispheres of the brain. These connections in turn lead to better communication and cognitive skills.

Moving the opposite hand and leg on the floor during crawling enhances your child's body rhythm and timing, which is important for skills that will later be required for maths and writing. It also encourages muscle development, especially of the hands, as your little one creeps along receiving sensory messages in the sensitive nerve endings of his outspread fingers.

Crawling also helps to develop your little one's eyes – the distance from floor to eyes when an infant is

crawling is the same as from page to eyes when reading, and focusing down at hands and then up at distant
objects is similar to shifting gaze from blackboard to book
at school age. So, if your one-year-old seems slower to get
up on her feet than another tot, don't push her. Instead,
remind yourself that she is developing strong foundations
for later learning.

Toddler tactic: encourage cross-patterning

*If your child is already walking but missed the crawling stage,
the brain pathways can still be established if you encourage
cross patterning through fun games such as crawling races
and making obstacle courses with cushions or large cardboard boxes as tunnels. Try placing one box in a doorway so
she is encouraged to crawl through the 'tunnel', or crawl round
the floor together pretending to be animals.*

Walking

Motor development takes place from the head down and
from the centre of the body outwards. Once your child has
developed control of his neck muscles, then his arms, back
and hips through crawling, the next step – literally – is to
balance upright and begin to walk.

To encourage walking skills:

❀ **Create a safe environment.** Make sure he has sturdy objects to pull himself up on, but try to resist holding his hands to help him balance until he is independently walking. He will develop better balance if he practises unaided most of the time.

❀ **Keep him on the level.** As your child learns to walk, it will take a while for him to develop the leg control and balance needed to stop, so give him plenty of opportunity to walk on flat (not sloping) surfaces so he doesn't have too many falls as he develops his walking skills. As your toddler grows more competent, walking up and down steps and slopes will help develop balance.

❀ **Bare feet are best.** Your little one receives sensory messages through the delicate nerve endings in her feet. Also, the foot bones are not fully formed until about eighteen months. Walking barefoot on different surfaces – grass, sand, carpet, concrete, tiles – will provide valuable tactile experience and help with body awareness and balance, as well as the development of tiny foot muscles. Bare feet help your child grip with her tiny toes and feet as she tries to balance. When she is walking steadily and is ready to wear shoes, have them properly fitted.

Toddler tactic: choose the right first shoes

Your toddler's first shoes should allow his feet the feeling and movement of 'barefootedness'. Soft leather booties are protective without being restrictive for one-year-olds who are just learning to walk. When your child is about eighteen months old and ready for 'real' shoes (bare feet are still best whenever it's practical), soles should be flexible enough that toes can bend comfortably.

Shoes should be roomy enough to allow for wriggling toes (check regularly as little feet grow quickly!), but should fit securely at the heels and have adjustable fastening and non-slip soles. Shoes with leather or canvas uppers and non-synthetic lining will absorb sweat and allow tiny feet to 'breathe'.

Running

Please don't push your little one to run too early (by chasing him, for instance), as too much pressure before he is ready can cause accidents. His top-heavy body and his inability to stop are likely to have him toppling over, rather than having fun. Be assured that as soon as your tot is ready to run, he will be so excited by this skill he will have you chasing just to keep up with him!

To give your toddler practice at learning to stop, play

music and dance, or do funny walks. As you stop and start the music, this is a signal to stop and start moving – a bit like playing statues except that a younger child won't be able to control his body enough to keep still.

Jumping

Before he can jump, your toddler needs lots of practice bobbing up and down, bending his knees to increase his awareness of his knees and legs. When he first tries to jump, he will often land with one foot after the other before he gains the skills to jump with both feet together. It is difficult for toddlers to coordinate their upper and lower body so they need support for their upper body as they begin to jump. Holding your child under his armpits or allowing him to hold a bed headboard while jumping on the mattress (supervised, of course) will be helpful. If the rule at your house is no jumping on beds, please consider that the urge to jump is innate and very strong, so it would be sensible to provide an old mattress or sofa cushions on the floor or outside so that children can jump safely. Later, a trampoline (under strict supervision) will be loads of fun – there are specially designed smaller trampolines for younger children. You can also encourage jumping over lines on footpaths, a hose across the lawn, or off small ledges and low fences as you are out walking.

Climbing

Do you remember going to the park and climbing on the jungle gym? Or climbing trees in the backyard? Although most toddlers start their climbing careers with a jaunt up onto the dining room table (and try not to shriek in shock the first time that happens!), there seems to be less and less time and freedom for small children to climb safely outdoors.

This is a pity because all that tree climbing, along with swinging and hanging from monkey bars and trees, helps children develop the upper body, arm and shoulder strength that precede the fine motor skills required for writing, painting and posting blocks into shape sorters. Climbing also helps develop hand–eye and eye–foot coordination, body control, muscle tone and cross patterning (opposite arm and leg movement), as well as spatial awareness and an understanding of concepts such as up, down, high and low. As your toddler begins to climb, teach him to turn around and climb down backwards feet first. With consistent repetition, he will eventually be able to climb safely – up and down!

Although you may feel a sense of panic as your little one climbs, it is important not to transmit your own fears, so mind your language and resist the urge to tell him not to fall. This could distract him and may even *cause* him to fall or lose confidence. If he is free to concentrate with you nearby to break his fall if necessary, he will attempt what he is reasonably capable of and will develop so much confidence you will soon be wondering if he has monkey glands.

As well as (or in preparation for) climbing, you can help develop upper-body coordination by playing 'wheelbarrows' with your toddler – supporting your child's body horizontally as she 'stands' or 'walks' on her hands – and by letting her hang and swing from bars or safe, smooth branches. Even a one-year-old can swing from a horizontal bar or a trapeze with support (hold him around his hips), but do teach your child to grip with his thumbs underneath the bar as this is a stronger, safer grip. Incidentally, it is also the correct way to hold a pencil later on.

Dancing

Put on some music and boogie with your toddler! As well as being great exercise, it's a no-mess activity that will get you both into a happy mood.

Here are some dance-related activities you might like to try:

❀ Make a music box full of fun props like scarves for dancing, simple shakers made from small jars of beans, rice or popcorn (glue the lids on tightly to prevent spillage and possible choking), bells on elastic to wear on legs and arms as you dance, a harmonica, chime bars, a recorder or a xylophone.

❀ Include rhythmic actions when you dance with your child. Encourage clapping, marching or stomping to the beat; tap your tot's knees and shoulders, bounce your child on your knee, facing you as you sing; make eye contact and be animated – your enthusiasm will be catching regardless of your talent (or lack of it!).

Rolling and spinning

Have you ever wondered why children love to roll down hills, swing upside down and spin around? This movement in all directions helps with development of the vestibular apparatus, a system of canals inside the inner ear covered in tiny hair-like structures called cilia. As fluid washes through these canals over the cilia, messages are sent to your child's brain helping him learn about balance. A child with an immature vestibular system and poor balance may be labelled as clumsy or he may fidget, wriggle, have trouble sitting still, or suffer from motion sickness.

To help stimulate your child's vestibular system, let him roll down hills, swing on swings and ride merry-go-rounds. Indoors, you can sit in an office chair and slowly spin your child, first one way, then the other; gently rotate him in a washing basket or turn on the spot as you give him a piggy back ride. Always spin back the other way to 'unwind' and remember that little and often is best – not more than a minute at a time.

You can help your toddler develop balance, coordination, muscle tone, and visual and auditory skills by giving lots of opportunities for physical activity. Here are some other ideas:

- ✿ Play with bubbles, letting your child watch, chase and catch them. You can use a tiny bubble wand or get a battery-operated machine – just make sure the bubble mix isn't overly perfumed.
- ✿ Encourage role-play and pretending. Encourage your child to try silly walks, crawling like an animal, dressing up and dancing.

🌼 For older toddlers, try hopscotch or Twister, riding scooters or tricycles, or jumping on small exercise trampolines. There are even books that show safe and easy yoga poses for children.

🌼 Hang up the car keys and walk to the park!

Chapter four
Behave yourself!

'Children require the most love and attention when they act the least deserving of it.'

Aletha Solter, psychologist

He wants it all. He wants it now. And he wants it all to himself! Your toddler can be affectionate one minute and obstinate the next. He runs away when you call him and yells when you want peace and quiet. He wants the blue cup, shirt or towel (whatever) when you offer him the yellow one. He seems to live on fresh air even though he's built like a tiny rugby player. It can take you all the energy and patience you can muster to enjoy your little adventurer as he learns about himself, other people and the whole big exciting world.

Now is the time to guide and protect your toddler with a new kind of parenting that includes setting appropriate limits: just as absolute freedom is confusing and can result in a child who is rejected socially because nobody likes an obnoxious brat, too many rules can make little ones feel so trapped that their only option is rebellion.

> *'Hattie loves to be in the kitchen with me. She is an independent little beastie, who will happily tinker at my feet but loves to get into the cupboards and fridge. Rather than have all the cupboards locked, I have filled the bottom drawer in the kitchen with small plastic containers and various interesting utensils. She proudly opens the drawer and helps herself to whatever takes her fancy, and I know she isn't into anything dangerous. I also have colourful fridge magnets in her reach on the fridge, and photos in magnet frames at her eye level. I try and focus on the things she can have rather than the things she can't.'*
>
> **Kate**

The good news is that setting limits becomes quite simple when we consider that the word 'discipline' is derived from the Latin word meaning 'to teach'. If you have given your sweet baby a gentle beginning and want to continue this with your approach to parenting a testing toddler, know that you can keep listening to your child and your heart while you employ kind and loving strategies that teach acceptable behaviour. One important thing to bear in mind is that creating family harmony and respectful children is not an overnight process. Learning to be 'good' is just like any other aspect of children's development. It takes time for little ones' bodies, brains and minds to develop the impulse control, physical agility and language skills that will help them control their childish whims and impish urges (at least, most of the time).

Creating a positive family environment will require lots of effort on your part but it will save a lot of energy and tension in the long run. The way we choose to treat our children, especially when their behaviour is challenging, will help them learn to get along with others, to deal with conflict and to problem solve. More importantly, it will help them develop neurological connections that will enable them to control impulses and react appropriately later on. This will enhance their relationships with us and with others, long beyond toddlerhood.

Your parenting toolbox

One way to work towards an atmosphere of harmony and cooperation is for you and your partner to sit down together and examine your parenting toolboxes.

We each have our own toolbox which is filled with strategies for getting through each day (relatively) sanely. These strategies have been collected and stashed away since we were children ourselves and may include the tactics our own parents used as well as the things we have learned from others along the way. It is up to each of us to examine what is useful and positive, what we want to pack in our toolbox and what doesn't fit.

To work out what we want in our parenting toolbox and what to discard, we need to be aware of our discipline style and our expectations (and what these are based on). We need to acknowledge what we are doing that isn't particularly effective or may be creating conflict within our family, and we need to be willing to consider new strategies. Parenting tools vary somewhat from one family to another, and because your partner will have had a different upbringing from yours, it is helpful to discuss your priorities and work things out as a team. As you define your family's discipline style and sort out your parenting toolbox, I suspect you will find it productive to discard tactics that set up power struggles and skill-up on ways to teach your child how you want him to behave that also foster connection and cooperation.

Let's have a look at the pros and cons of some common tools that parents use to enlist cooperation from children (read, make kids behave).

Smacking

A recent Australian study undertaken by *Choice* magazine showed that about 80 per cent of mothers (and 90 per cent of mothers under twenty-five) believed that smacking was acceptable. Any one of us can be pushed to our limits when we are confronted by toddler mayhem, but smacking really isn't a useful option to include in your toolbox.

According to other studies into the effects of physical punishment, although children may comply in the short term, they do not learn the desired behaviour (remember, discipline means 'to teach'). It is highly likely that as your children push the boundaries further, you'll find yourself hitting harder as your frustration levels escalate. There is also increasing evidence to suggest that physical punishment may be linked with more aggressive or antisocial behaviour, emotional damage and diminished cognitive ability. In a review of several longitudinal studies published in *The Psychologist* in 2002, psychologist Dr Penelope Leach found smacking related to a five-fold increase in toddler non-compliance; a four-fold increase in assaults on siblings by children under ten; double the rate of physical aggression in school playgrounds among six-year-olds; and an increased likelihood of substance abuse and criminal convictions in adolescence.

People justify smacking in lots of ways. Some say the Bible advises smacking, and use the quote 'spare the rod and spoil the child' (actually, the shepherd used his rod to *guide* the sheep, he didn't hit them with it). Others equate discipline with punishment and think that if they don't smack their children, they aren't disciplining them. But we *can* set boundaries and teach children good behaviour without hitting them. In fact, most of us would label a child who hits another child a bully, or a teenager who thumps somebody a thug, and an adult who slaps a workmate or (heaven forbid!) their partner would be regarded with absolute horror and probably receive a criminal conviction. So why is it acceptable for adults to hit small children? At what age does hitting a person become assault – when they are eighteen and an adult, for instance?

To me, the issue of smacking is rather like learning a second language: most parents were brought up being smacked, so unless we have other strategies to replace smacking, under stress we will revert to our 'mother tongue' and lash out at our children. This may only happen in extreme circumstances (such as when a child runs onto a road, for instance), but if we learn and demonstrate positive strategies (such as making it a rule to hold a grown-up's hand near the road), our children will learn new ways to care for their own children. Then, smacking will not be included in *their* parenting toolboxes and their automatic response will be a more gentle, empathetic approach.

> *'Before we had kids my mother tried to convince me that you could not raise children without hitting them. I think I have proven conclusively that you can!*
>
> *'We don't believe in ridiculing or hitting, so gentle discipline was really the only option for us. I find myself repeating, "There's one mummy and two babies," about a thousand times a day but I believe it helps the kids understand when I am stretched and need their help.*
>
> *'We're very verbal – I explain everything as thoroughly as I can since I believe the kids understand a lot more than society gives them credit for. As a result, I usually get cooperation pretty easily. We also have a no shouting rule though there are times when Euan, who's three, needs to remind me to use my inside voice as I revert, on occasion, to what I experienced as a child.'*
>
> **Mandy**

Time out

So, if you aren't going to smack, what then? Should you try 'time out'? This depends on how you interpret the concept and what you hope to teach your child. If time out involves physically isolating your child, it isn't appropriate for a child under three, since the stress of separation anxiety can be overwhelming to a toddler who is already having difficulty with out-of-control feelings. All you are likely to teach your little one is that it is unacceptable to express difficult emotions: learning to suppress his feelings through fear of being isolated is likely to result in more episodes of bad behaviour later on because your child's underlying needs haven't been addressed.

According to psychotherapist and infant mental health specialist Margot Sunderland, by supporting your tot and teaching him how to calm down when he is frustrated or upset, you are helping establish important brain pathways for managing stress and being assertive in later life. Therefore, a more positive way to interpret 'time out' for toddlers is to take them away from a situation that seems overwhelming and give them a break until they settle – remaining with them to help them deal with their big feelings. It is fine to soothe children and hold them firmly but calmly (remember, the aim is to teach them emotional regulation and your own example is very powerful) if they are raging.

If toddler behaviour has been unacceptable or unsafe,

such as hurting another child, it is appropriate to tell little ones what you do want them to do as they settle (there is no point trying to reason with an out-of-control child), then offer a diversion as you take them back to play. A good rule after taking time out is 'when it is over, it is over' – your child doesn't need reminders of his mistakes.

Bribes and rewards

'If you sit on the potty, you can have a Smartie.'

'Thank you for helping pack up the toys. Now we can go to the park.'

'I will get you the ice-cream now if you promise you will sit still in the doctor's room.'

What is the difference between a bribe and a reward? A bribe is something offered *before* the task in order to get your child to do what you want him to do (so the first and third example are bribes). A reward (the second example) is something that happens after the event.

Does it matter, as long as it makes your child cooperate? Well, that depends on what you are trying to teach him. Do you want a child who will only do things if there is something in it for him? Do you want to encourage your child to have an unreasonable sense of entitlement, to ask himself, 'What's in it for me?' each time there is a job to be done? Or would you like to teach your child that when he cooperates or works hard, he will feel satisfied by a job well done? That work comes before play? That it is good to consider everybody's needs? And that because your tot has helped you, you feel pleased with him and perhaps now have energy and time to spend with him? Of course, some of these goals are beyond a toddler's capacity to understand, but it is worth setting a pattern and developing a family culture around positive values.

Any one of us in a hurry or desperate to motivate our child can resort to bribery or rewards (or is that offering incentives?), but it does pay to be cautious about our own motivation and methods. It is perfectly reasonable to say, 'When you are in your pyjamas we will have a story,' or 'When the toys are packed away, we can go to the park,' but offering bribes, especially material goods, every time we want to enlist cooperation is likely to backfire. Looking at the examples above, offering Smarties could cause your child to race to the potty every few minutes in order to get a treat, rather than learning to actually *use* the potty. And an ice-cream delivered before a visit to the doctor won't motivate any child to live up to his promise of cooperation – he has the prize, what does it matter? Besides, a toddler lives in the present: he doesn't have the cognitive skills or impulse control required to think ahead, so he can't be held to a promise, whatever the incentive. Apart from the fact that children become wise and are likely to raise the stakes for bribery and rewards (read, ask for bigger incentives as they grow – imagine offering a Play-Station if they kick a goal in their footy match!), they may eventually refuse to do a single thing unless there is something in it for them. Also, if you constantly give rewards for good behaviour or achievements, then one day when you don't give a reward, your child may give up and stop trying. Even worse, when a reward is attached to every achievement, we devalue our child's efforts because we are subtly telling him we didn't think he was up to the task, and this is no help to his self-esteem.

At least most of the time, it's best to allow your child to have the satisfaction of achieving a goal by simply acknowledging his efforts. Occasionally, you could offer a small reward that is a natural consequence of his cooperation. There is another principle at work here, too – psychologists call it 'intermittent reinforcement', which means that giving occasional rewards as a surprise works better from a behavioural perspective than having your child expect a reward each time he does something wonderful.

Being mindful of rewards (for effort, rather than

achievement) and bribery (which comes before the deed so can have trade-offs, especially in the longer term) means that your child will be more likely to strive because he will be intrinsically motivated.

Praise

Praise is a positive strategy, isn't it? We like recognition for a job well done, and so do children. It is perfectly natural to delight in every little thing your toddler does – he is cute and funny and is doing new tricks every single day, so how can you resist telling your child how clever he is?

Just as with rewards, be cautious with praise. While a spontaneous, 'Wow! What a clever kid!' won't do any harm, if you heap on the praise for every breath your child takes, you run the risk of setting up a 'great expectations' trap. This can mean that, as your child grows, he feels he has to keep performing to be accepted and loved. This can contribute to a fear of failure, which may mean that your child is so dependent on the approval of others that he may be afraid to try new things. So, instead of gushing, 'What a lovely painting!' it is better to offer realistic compliments: admire the bright blue sky or the very wiggly lines or tell your child, 'What a lot of colours you have used, I can't wait to hang this up on the wall.'

Another positive way to offer praise without overdoing it is a process called 'mirroring' which involves naming exactly what a child has done. By mirroring back to your child what he or she has done ('You have climbed five steps on the ladder, all by yourself!', 'You sat very quietly while I was talking to the nurse'), you are giving them tangible evidence of their efforts, not just empty words that may or may not be believable to them. You can extend mirroring to include a quality: 'You are so *patient* for letting me talk without interrupting.' Other examples could be: 'Thank you for remembering to shut the car door. That was very *responsible*,' or 'Good sharing, that is so *kind*.' This helps nourish your child's identity so that he will begin to think of himself as a genuinely competent person, seeing himself as kind, responsible, generous, helpful, funny, strong and whatever other positive labels you choose to describe his efforts.

This positive praise is far more powerful than empty praise that can see your child undermined the first time another child says, 'What a dumb block tower.' Because your child will have tangible evidence that he really is competent, his self-esteem will not be dependent on constant recognition and he won't crumple like a stack of blocks with the slightest hint of disapproval.

Another small but important caution about dishing out praise is to remember to notice your child 'being good'. How often do we ignore 'good' (read, convenient) behaviour but notice the smallest mistake?

Teaching 'good' behaviour

By looking at your child's behaviour as communication or an attempt to connect with you, and considering the emotion or need behind the behaviour, you will be setting up a strong foundation for positive discipline. Your child will develop a sense of what is right or wrong that doesn't depend on having the Mummy or Daddy police there to constantly correct him. He will try his best to do the right thing because he cares about people and his environment, not because he might be caught in the act, and his relationship with you will be more respectful because of your own conscious and considerate modelling.

'I believe that kids mostly want to do the right thing and want to please you, and this belief helps me with gentle discipline. I try to teach the right way to behave rather than punish for acting the wrong way. For aggressive behaviour, I usually tell the kids that that action would be hurting the other child and that we

need to be gentle with other people. Then, depending on their age, I either tell them, "This is how to be gentle," and use their hand to stroke the arm of the other child, or (for older children), "Show me how you can be gentle." Then I say, "Well done," or "I knew you could do it." For repeated misbehaviour or refusing to do something I have asked them to do (like getting dressed because we are going out), my kids know that a few minutes in the corner is their other choice. It's completely up to them.

'They are usually happy to behave as expected as long as I don't expect too much. Expecting them to jump the second after I ask them to do something is unfair and very military-like. I try to wait until after their favourite show on TV finishes or is in an ad break or a game has finished to ask them to come to dinner. My daughter will sometimes say, "Just a minute, Mummy," and if my request is not urgent I reply, "Okay," or I tell her, "No, I need you to come now please." It's a matter of respect. I can't jump to their requests every time and I think it's only fair the other way round, too. I think using manners when speaking to your children is important. I can't expect my kids to learn the correct behaviour if I don't use it myself.'

Sonia

Your role as teacher of a toddler can be a challenge – at this stage you aren't dealing with a potentially reasonable, miniature adult. Toddlers have short attention spans, immature nervous systems (they may be overstimulated by exposure to background noise such as television or bright lighting, so shopping centres can be overwhelming), emotional needs that aren't easy to articulate with a limited vocabulary, and a variety of physical needs (hunger, tiredness, food allergies or sensitivities to substances such as sugar, caffeine, chemicals), as well as insatiable curiosity. These factors all affect little ones' behaviour.

Another important factor to consider when we want children to 'be good' is that there is a vast difference between what we can expect from a one-year-old in comparison to a three-year-old. Just as your child can't be expected to walk until he has the appropriate physical coordination, the ability to 'behave' is influenced by developmental readiness, especially neurological development. This isn't a reflection of your little one's intelligence, but is related to brain connections that enable behaviour such as impulse control which means your child can stop himself from doing things that are unsafe or unacceptable. Each child will develop at his own rate, but being aware of what to reasonably expect at each stage can help you be more realistic and may save unnecessary battles.

Your **one-year-old** is ruled by insatiable curiosity and

has barely any impulse control. He is likely to be clingy as his separation anxiety peaks at about this age. He may mutter 'no' as he reaches for something he isn't allowed but he probably won't be able to stop himself from grabbing it. Social niceties such as manners and sharing are well beyond his language development and his cognitive capacity so, at this stage, careful supervision and distraction work best to divert him from trouble. Keep breakables out of reach or offer an alternative (a torch if he is besotted with switches, photos in empty CD cases instead of glass photo frames) and protect him from potential hazards such as heaters or electrical sockets by installing safety guards and caps.

At **two years old**, your child may still be clingy when he is in unfamiliar places or with new people so will need support to become confident in new situations. He can be emotional and may cry easily – this doesn't mean you should 'toughen him up' by not responding. These tears will pass as your toddler learns words to express his feelings. Meanwhile, a hug and a Band Aid without too much fuss will usually fix most 'ouchies'.

Tantrums are common but usually only around people your child knows very well. Don't feel like a bad parent if your mother-in-law tells you he doesn't have tantrums for her! This just means your child feels safer to let out his feelings with you and you can take this as a positive. It isn't healthy for children to be 'emotionally promiscuous' which includes hugging strangers (of course, Grandma isn't a stranger and is entitled to hugs if your child feels okay about this, though he does have a right to refuse unwanted touching). Often tears and tantrums happen because your two-year-old is insisting on doing things for himself but isn't realistic about what he can manage so he becomes upset when things don't work out.

Two-year-olds enjoy being with other tots and will start to share but they may snatch toys and can be quite rough. This isn't usually intentional but is often due to sensory immaturity. Your toddler may feel other children are too close for comfort. Because his peripheral vision is limited, your toddler may not notice other children until they are suddenly upon him grabbing 'his' things. Show him how to be gentle and that hurting people isn't accept-able. Teach him how to use his words by practising with him so he is more likely to remember when he is feeling threatened.

At **three years old**, children are usually happy to be left in a familiar place but some tots may still be clingy. It is counterproductive to force your child to be 'independent' so respect her needs for support. Tantrums happen less often and they are more predictable as your child's mood changes when she is about to 'explode'. The good news is that she will probably be sorry afterwards.

Although she is more able to respect 'family rules', there can be a few battles as your three-year-old likes to choose what she wears (pyjamas seem to be most comfortable!) and what she eats. Although she likes being with other children, your child's protectiveness towards her belongings means she may share on neutral territory such as kindergarten, but not at home. If she is having a play date, ask her to choose what she would like to put away before visitors come, then she can be expected and encouraged to share what is left out.

'My partner, Matt, had bravely decided to take our three-year-old son and one-year-old daughter shopping at a local supermarket. With Eve perched happily in the kiddy seat of the trolley, Matt only had Lloyd to manage. The little bloke, clutching his favourite stuffed toy – Monkey – was willing to oblige for about half the length of the biscuits and cereals aisle, but then found the open space and shiny floor irresistible. 'Here, Dad,' he said, passing Monkey to his father, and took off, disappearing around the end of the aisle with a squeal of delight.

'Matt didn't batt an eyelid. Calmly, he wheeled the trolley to where Lloyd could see him, and held Monkey high in one hand. "Lloyd!" he said in his best police officer voice. The little boy stopped still, as did most of the checkout staff in the supermarket. "Stop! Or the monkey gets it!" Matt said. Lloyd screamed "No!" and ran straight back to his father, much to the amused grins of the staff.'

Miriam

Setting limits

Toddlers learn the limits by testing them. It is normal for toddlers to assert their developing independence by saying no or 'escaping'. This doesn't mean you will thwart their development by setting limits. In fact, now is the time to gently lay the foundations of discipline.

❀ **Keep expectations realistic.** Toddlers don't understand concepts like hurry, tidy and wait, and taking turns or sharing depend on developmental readiness, not parental demands. Keep teaching, but be patient.

❀ **Notice the good things.** Toddlers like to please the people they love, and they delight in attention. Comment positively and give hugs when you notice good behaviour and you will get more of it. (See Praise, page 70.)

❀ **Mind your tone.** Your voice affects the atmosphere and your child's willingness to listen and comply, so please don't plead, nag or shout. Instead, try to be calm and positive. Take a few deep breaths if your buttons are being pushed and make requests without sounding like you are attacking: 'Blocks are for building' (not throwing); 'Tables are for eating at' (not climbing); 'We only bite food' (not people). You may need to physically redirect a strong-willed child (read, scoop him off the table and offer a diversion) as you speak calmly but firmly.

❀ **Acknowledge your child's feelings.** Different parts of the brain are involved in emotions and speech, so being able to express his feelings in words (rather than physically) will take a few years and developmental readiness.

However, giving your child words and showing him he is being listened to is likely to minimise physical aggression. When little ones feel understood and, later, can talk about feelings, it is easier to release pent-up stress without resorting to kiddy violence.

❀ **Give clear instructions.** Telling children what you *do* want is more effective than telling them what not to do – 'Hold my hand,' is better than 'Don't run on the road.' And 'Use your spoon,' works better than 'Don't eat with your fingers.' For some reason, little ones only seem to hear the actual request, not the 'don't' that comes first.

Even a one-year-old can follow very simple instructions if you present these clearly with lots of repetition. You will also need to demonstrate what you want and set a physical boundary. For instance, you can say, 'Safe, safe,' to your twelve-month-old as you turn his body so he learns to go down steps backwards rather than head-first. Later, you will just have to remind him with words as you supervise. A toddler of eighteen months who is a little 'escape artist' will need to have his hand held as you tell him to 'hold hands'. If there is a threat such as a busy road, always take the initiative of holding your toddler's hand as you give an instruction, whatever his age.

❀ **Limit rules.** Children learn the rules more quickly when there aren't too many of them: the more you say no, the less effective it becomes. And if we keep changing our minds on the little 'nos', kids learn not to take us seriously on the big 'NO!' Make the environment as safe as possible, so that no can be saved for things that really matter. And be sure to follow through: if your resistance is low and you know you will probably give in to a request, it is better to say yes in the first place, than to change your mind for peace.

❀ **Say yes more than no.** Your child is a mimic – too many 'nos' could have a little tike whose favourite (and most powerful) word is no. When your child asks for a biscuit, instead of saying no you could try, 'Yes, after dinner.' Or instead of 'No TV,' try, 'We can watch TV when all the toys are packed away.'

❀ **Create a diversion.** Divert your toddler from potentially harmful or dangerous situations (or things that simply drive you bananas) by giving her something more acceptable to play with. For instance, if she likes to fiddle with TV knobs, remove her from the vicinity and try offering her a torch to switch off and on. If she is fascinated with photos in frames, give her some photos of special people or pets in empty CD cases. If she jumps on the sofa or bed and this is against your household rules, provide an acceptable jumping place, such as an old mattress on the floor or a trampoline outside.

❀ **Limit choices.** Offering choices helps your child to become a decision-maker and think for himself. This helps develop self-esteem and enlists cooperation. Don't, however, offer open-ended choices or your child will be confused. Above all, make sure the options you offer suit *you*! Instead of asking, 'What do you want to wear?' say, 'Would you like to wear your red shirt or the blue one with cars on?' Or, at snack time, 'Would you like a banana or a pear?'(this way, there is no room for him to request junk food). And, when you are out and he is getting feisty, ask, 'Would you like to ride in the stroller or hold my hand?'

❀ **Think ahead.** It is better to prevent trouble than react angrily later. For instance, put folded washing out of sight if you don't want it thrown out of the basket or tracked around the house, and prevent precious things being broken by banning ball-throwing inside and keeping the balls outside.

❀ **Be flexible.** Try to see things from your child's perspective. If your little one is engrossed in an activity, perhaps give her a bit longer to complete her game or give her a few minutes' notice before you zip her off to go shopping, call her inside for dinner or scoop her up for a bath, for instance.

❀ **Think of 'mistakes' as opportunities to teach your child to make amends.** Instead of yelling or muttering under heavy breath as you clean up an accidental mess, try to problem-solve by saying, 'The book is torn, how can we fix it?' or 'Oops, the milk spilt. If I get the sponge, can you help me wipe it up, please?' This way, instead of seeing himself as a klutz or naughty or thinking that Mummy or Daddy will fix things when he mucks up, you are teaching your child to take responsibility for his mistakes.

✿ **Practise what you preach.** If you expect good manners, use them yourself. If you expect children to pick up their toys, put your own things away. Children learn best by imitation – the good and the bad!

✿ **Create a safe, child-friendly environment.** It is much easier and less stressful to care for a toddler in a child-proof home and backyard that caters to his needs for exploration and play. Remember, little explorers move very quickly, have limited impulse control and absolutely no sense of danger. So, if you don't want the cat covered in Vicks VapoRub, the car painted or a trip to the hospital, please store everything you don't want explored safely out of reach (from precious breakables to medicines, cleaning products and garden tools).

Tears and tantrums

If you have ever watched a desperate mother trying to avoid flailing arms and legs as she wipes her child's snot off her arms in the middle of a shopping centre and vowed that your own sweet baby will never carry on like that, think again. Tantrums are a normal part of toddler life. It can help to think of a tantrum as an intense storm of emotion that a toddler isn't equipped to handle, rather than an attempt to wield power over everyone around him.

Tantrums are often an expression of emotional distress and can be triggered by frustration, loss, disappointment, feeling misunderstood or a need to discharge an accumulation of stress. Of course, some tantrums are about pushing boundaries, perhaps to get the biscuit or toy that isn't allowed. These outbursts are usually fairly easily diverted or will blow over if they are ignored (with you close by). But do consider whether the 'biscuit tantrum' is actually the straw that broke the camel's back – is your child's seemingly massive reaction really about the biscuit or an accumulation of minor but stressful events that have happened to her throughout the day (a spilt drink at breakfast, her brother knocking over her block tower, waiting for lunch while Mummy settled the crying baby) or the result of tiredness or low blood sugar?

By trying to see things from your child's perspective, it is much easier not to take tantrums personally, and it will be much easier to help your little one grow through this stage relatively smoothly than if you turn every outburst into a power struggle. Each time you help your child deal with his intense emotions, console yourself that you are sculpting stress-regulating mechanisms in his tiny brain that will enable him to deal with frustration and rage in later life. According to Dr Margot Sunderland, the too-good child who does not have tantrums may have learned early on that expressing big feelings elicits a frightening parental response, and that the price of parental love is total compliance. She explains that the too-good child misses out on vital brain sculpting, meaning that when he faces frustration in later life, he may respond with angry outbursts or struggle to be assertive.

'During tantrums, if we are out, I physically hold my toddlers to keep them safe. I ignore protests and promptly remove them, explaining that we simply cannot tolerate that behaviour and as a result it is time to go. We also talk gently to our kids: "Mummy knows that you are angry and tired but this behaviour is not acceptable." It is also important when the episode is over and you know that your child has understood to ask them if they need a cuddle. They are usually desperate for some tenderness (as deep down I think it is simply strong emotions and confusion that cause the undesirable behaviour), and once their behaviour is back in line it is crucial to reward them for the positive change.'

Marie

Taming tantrums

You can reduce tantrums and help your child (and you) cope better with stressful situations by using some simple strategies and sensible planning:

✿ **Eliminate frustration beyond your toddler's limits.** Challenges are necessary for children to develop, but try to step in before a challenge becomes a frustration. Guide gently, but don't take over. For instance, discreetly turn the puzzle piece over so he can put it in by himself. When you sense your tot is reaching the brink, create a diversion towards a calming, soothing activity – a different place, a toy, a hug, a story, a song or perhaps a snack.

✿ **Look for triggers.** Do tantrums seem to happen mostly when your tot is tired, hungry or rushed? Are there situations he finds difficult to handle such as playgroup, shopping or being strapped in a car seat? Keeping a tantrum diary might help you understand triggers. Try to think ahead and limit overwhelming situations. For instance, plan short shopping trips when he isn't tired, take nutritious snacks and water whenever you go out, and don't wait for difficult behaviour before you offer food or it can seem like a reward.

❀ **Cut out junk food.** Some foods can make little angels morph into complete rascals: sweets can trigger blood sugar variations that cause mood swings; caffeine in drinks can hype kids up for hours (toddlers should never have 'cola' drinks, and that goes for Diet Coke too), so they are literally unable to sit still, let alone fall asleep; and additives in foods (even many that are normally considered healthy), can affect some sensitive tots. Again, a tantrum diary might shed light on food triggers. (See also Let's eat, page 175.)

❀ **Listen respectfully.** Imagine the frustration of a little child who can't express what he is trying to tell you. Is it any wonder he 'loses it' when he doesn't feel heard by the important people in his life – you would too, wouldn't you? Listen carefully to what your toddler is trying to say, just as you would with another adult. Reflect back your child's feelings so that he feels heard and understood. Say, 'You look angry that your block tower crashed,' or 'I get angry too, when I can't have what I want.'

❀ **Choose your battles.** Don't sweat the small things is a good rule for parents. Save your energy for the things that really matter and avoid power struggles (it doesn't matter, for instance, if your child insists on having her cereal in the pink bowl or wears gumboots with her party dress). Allowing her a little independence on small things can help your child feel in control, and she may then be more flexible on the things that do matter. Rules like seat belts and holding hands near roads are not negotiable, but a balance between health and safety and a happy day can benefit family relationships. So take a peek at things from your child's perspective (imagine how you would feel if somebody told you how to dress or messed up your morning ritual), childproof your home, and keep rules for important things.

❀ **Say no and mean it.** It's far better to say yes initially than to change your mind after your child has exploded. Remember, 'maybe' means 'yes' to a child. Rewarding genuinely uncontrollable tantrums can encourage tots to use (semi)deliberate tantrums to get what they want.

❀ **Don't give in to embarrassment.** It can be difficult to consider your child's feelings when he performs a tantrum in public but whatever you do, don't yell back, don't smack and don't give in because you feel embarrassed. And please, don't walk away from an unruly tot in places like shopping centres. It is scary enough to be out of control without also feeling abandoned. The best thing you can do is scoop up your child and leave.

'We were in a shop when I refused to buy a sweet for my two-and-a-half-year-old. She threw herself on the ground and started screaming and kicking. There were old biddies all around staring and muttering, so I made an announcement: "My child is having a tantrum and I am choosing to ignore her."'

Sue

✿ **Offer comfort.** Because you know your child best, you'll know whether this is a 'tiny tanty' or a major blow-out, and whether he is better letting off steam by himself (with you nearby) or whether he needs to be removed from an overwhelming situation and held firmly but calmly. If your child is thrashing wildly and at risk of hurting himself or others, you can help him by using a technique known as 'holding'. This will only work if you can keep yourself calm – the idea isn't to restrain your child, but to help him feel secure and emotionally held.

Sit against a wall, if possible, to support your back, and breathe deeply to calm yourself. Psychotherapist Dr Margot Sunderland advises: 'Visualise yourself as a lovely warm, calm blanket.' Now envelop your child by holding him with his back to you (if he kicks, he will be kicking away from you) and folding your arms over his. If he is a bigger toddler, take an arm in each of your hands and cross his arms. You can also cross your legs over his to contain his legs and prevent kicking. Hold him calmly and use a gentle tone to say soothing words ('It's all right, I am going to hold you until you calm down'), allowing him to release his angry feelings. He won't be in any space to reason with and will, in any case, not be able to activate the reasoning part of his brain while he is distressed. As your tot calms, let him lie in your arms and cuddle until he is over his blow-out. Then offer him reassurance and a different, preferably quiet, activity.

If you find walking away works for your child during a fairly mild tantrum, return when he settles, hug him and say, 'I'm still here and I love you.' Giving reassurance is not giving in. Just as adults need comfort when they feel upset or overwhelmed, toddlers need to know they are loved, even when their behaviour isn't lovable, and by hugging him when he is calm you are rewarding him for settling down. By showing your child that you are in charge, he will feel secure and safe enough to let out his feelings and then move on.

✿ **Express your own feelings appropriately.** Supporting your child's emotional fallouts goes hand in hand with acknowledging and expressing your own feelings appropriately and honestly. It can also help to think about which of your child's feelings you have the most difficulty dealing with, and to try to understand your child's perspective by trying to recall your own feelings as a child. Think of a time when you felt upset as a child and the response of adults in your world was unsupportive. Were you belittled for crying? Punished for expressing anger? Now, imagine how you would have liked to be treated.

Emotional Intelligence, or EI, has become somewhat of a buzzword in corporate circles where it is a highly valued quality. The basic attributes of emotional intelligence are: awareness of one's feelings and the ability to control them; emotional resilience and ability to perform consistently; motivation with the drive and energy to achieve results; sensitivity to others' needs and the ability to change and influence others; decisiveness; integrity and conscientiousness.

This all sounds a far cry from the world of the toddler who may struggle with the basics of separation anxiety, taking turns and sharing. But your understanding of your child's emotional milestones, along with your ability to show empathy (put yourself in your child's shoes and see her perspective), will form the foundations for later emotional intelligence. How you support your child to express his or her feelings in these early years is important too. It can take a lot of practice to react calmly to a very emotional child, but whether she is having a meltdown because she can't get her shoes on or has broken a precious toy, if you acknowledge your toddler's feelings with understanding words, rather than dismissing her sadness or frustration, you can make a difference to how she deals with these strong feelings. This will have long-term effects: when we teach children that their feelings count, that we will respond to them, that there are people who they can trust and rely on to be sensitive to them, they learn that it is safe for them to be open and expressive, and to ask for what they need. This is emotional intelligence.

'I'm still working on the tantrums – mine! We don't hit or smack in this house, and I try to refrain from yelling. The kids are a good guide to how I'm going, because I see them act towards each other the way I act towards them. When I hear them yelling at each other I know I need to watch myself. When I hear them being polite and understanding to each other, I know I'm doing pretty well. We don't do time out either, apart from when

I need a five-minute break from them to regain my composure. All in all, I think I must be doing something right because my kids are happy and treat others well.'

Zoe

Sharing

Do you lend your friends your car, your computer or your brand-new shoes? Isn't it a bit unrealistic, then, to expect your toddler to willingly part with his favourite toys whenever a strange child visits?

Being able to share is a developmental stage that most children under three simply aren't ready to manage. Sharing requires quite a few learning steps and lots of patient teaching along the way: before a tot can share, she has to learn what 'mine' means. The discovery of this magical word heralds your child's awareness that there are some things she can move, control and keep. Later, she learns that she can share something that belongs to her without losing it forever.

To encourage sharing:

❀ If a toy is special, don't expect your child to share it, even if she has learned the meaning of sharing and taking turns. If you are expecting visitors, help your child put away special toys he finds difficult to share. It can be helpful to bring out 'sharing' toys such as blocks and balls, and play with little ones or stay close and keep them on track as they get used to new friends, so play dates aren't fraught with squabbles.

✿ Talk about which toys your child is happy to share as you introduce the idea of taking turns ('Share for a little while'), then acknowledge and praise your child's efforts ('Good sharing, that is really kind!') when he does share.

✿ Teach your toddler about sharing by exaggerating your own behaviour – 'Mummy is sharing her orange with Daddy.' You can also use encouraging language ('It tastes better when we share') as you divide food. As toddlers get a little older, encourage sharing food by allowing one child to divide and the other to have first choice. This will soon see the chocolate bar meticulously divided down to the last crumb!

Aggression

When your lovingly parented, gently reared tot is hit, scratched or (horror of horrors!) bitten by some other parent's uncontrollable little thug, it is only natural to shoot a pious glance at the perpetrator's parent as you swoop to rescue your sweet, screaming child. Of course, if it is your child who is committing the violence, it can be even more distressing to find yourself the recipient of judgmental glares. Be assured that most toddlers resort to the odd bout of aggressive behaviour at some stage.

One-year-old toddlers aren't really able to differentiate between people (who have feelings) and objects (that don't hurt when pushed or munched on). A moving person is intriguing – the tiny tot wants to know what they are made of and how they work, and another small person at his eye level is a real temptation to grab, poke or taste.

Generally, **two-year-olds** outgrow this exploratory biting and pushing, and aggression may be due to other factors. Toddlers may bite or shove out of frustration: without language skills, there aren't a whole lot of options for expressing exactly what you want (especially if another child has it) or that you are feeling overwhelmed by the world, so the nearest kid cops it!

Even **three-year-olds** can be aggressive and push others if they aren't confident with language. This tends to apply more to boys than girls, who are often more articulate at a younger age. It can help to give children specific signals to use – teach them to put their hand up as they loudly say, 'Stop!' if they don't like what another child is doing so they don't have to resort to violence.

In most cases there is no malice intended by the child who is biting or hitting. Their behaviour may be due to undeveloped impulse control combined with an immature nervous system, or the fact that pushing hard or chomping down simply *feels* good (especially if the biter is teething).

If your child seems to be playing roughly and you can't work out what is triggering this behaviour, she may be helped to overcome her 'roughness' by being offered more sensory experiences such as massage and a range of sensory play such as climbing and playing in sand and, of course, close supervision until she learns the rules about playing 'nicely'.

'Much to my horror, at the age of eighteen months, Jed turned into a biter. Usually he would bite when he got too excited or if someone (usually his older sister) took something off him, or held it above his head or out of reach. He also used to grab toys and hit people over the head with them. It was terrible. When I went to places with other children, I had to tail Jed everywhere in case he would attack someone. Going to my

regular breastfeeding support group get-togethers was not relaxing any more. He even bit another child at daycare on two occasions.

'All I could do was to keep saying "gentle" while showing him a patting motion. He would repeat this, then the patting would become more frenzied, then it would turn into a full-on hit. This behaviour continued for about nine months, then it finally started to ease. Looking back, it probably coincided with his speech development. His language skills were excellent, and as he learned to communicate more freely, the aggressive behaviour slowed down. Now he's two-and-a-half and I find I can relax a bit more and am starting to enjoy the company of other mums with young children again.'

Simone

Some children have difficulty integrating sensory messages. They may not be able to process the messages that their body is sending to their brain and may, as a result, act aggressively or inappropriately. He may, for example, have difficulty standing in line or sitting in a group close to other children because he will be touching everyone, or he will complain that everyone is touching him. He might perceive a touch from another child as a shove and lash out, or he may complain about his clothing (or strip off!).

This is often the child who insists on wearing his socks inside out because the seams are bothering him, or refuses to wear clothes made from certain fabrics or with tags that irritate him.

Be patient about clothing choices. Older, worn clothes will be more comfortable than stiff new ones; natural fabrics will be less irritating; plain socks rather than patterned ones will have fewer potentially scratchy threads inside them; and if your child wants to wear his socks inside out, let him. Also, remove tags from inside clothes and choose a low-irritant washing powder to avoid itching.

Another child may need to be able to touch something so he can actually stop still long enough to concentrate. In this case, you could try offering him a small textured ball, a key ring or something that vibrates so when he needs to, he can simply reach into his pocket and play with his touchy-feely toy.

As your toddler's social scene expands, you can expect a few squabbles but serious fisticuffs can be minimised.

❀ Keep a close eye on toddlers while they play together.
❀ Consider, does your child tend to bite or push when he plays with a large number of children (for example, at playgroup or a large indoor play-centre)? Is he better

at playing with just one or two little friends? Younger toddlers, especially, may find large group play overwhelming or the environment itself overstimulating. If that's the case for your toddler, organise play dates with just one or two children until your child can manage better. You could also try shortening the time spent in large group situations or perhaps make them outdoors (at a park, for instance), so your child is less likely to feel crowded.

❀ You don't need to intervene in every little disagreement. This is how children eventually learn to sort things out for themselves. When you do intervene, don't make a fuss. Gently remove the child who is doing the hurting from play for a little while. Hold him calmly (but not too tightly – remember you are modelling self-control) as you help him settle down or release pent-up feelings. Resist telling him he is 'naughty' (or whatever label might come to mind in the heat of the moment) – it is his *behaviour* that is unacceptable.

❀ Ideally, you will be watchful enough to catch a child before he bites or hits and you can quietly stop him and divert him. There is no point entering a battle between two toddlers. A new game can help everyone settle down.

❀ Remember that toddlers learn by copying. If shouts and smacks are the way you settle disagreements at home, don't be surprised if your child smacks another little playmate. The same goes for biting – please don't bite a biter. It won't show him how it feels for others because, at this stage, he really can't process that. However, it will almost certainly show him that it's okay for you, therefore it should be okay for him. As the saying goes, violence begets violence.

❀ Try to maintain perspective: what looks like extreme violence to adults probably doesn't have very much, if any, malicious intent to a toddler and the less fuss the adults present make, the sooner little ones will become friends again. By teaching toddlers how to be gentle, they will eventually learn to play nicely without beating up on their playmates.

'When our little girl is aggressive to her baby brother, we remove him from the situation rather than expect her to stop, but while doing so we explain to her that we would never let anybody hurt her and we cannot let her hurt her brother. We think it's important to understand where the aggression comes from, in order to handle it better. For example, has she recently played with another child who is going through an aggressive stage?

If so, we will avoid that situation until the stage has passed. If the aggression is due to tiredness, then a sleep will fix the problem. Sometimes a discomfort such as hunger or a need to go to the toilet can bring out aggression. Sometimes, aggression is simply another stage to go through. When she finds it funny to hurt people, a brush off with "ouch" and walking away fixes it, because if she gets no reaction it is not interesting enough to keep trying.'

Linda

'In situations where there is aggression shown to other children I have said, "No!" and separated them from the other kids. But it's always been a one-chance-only thing. The second time the action was repeated we have left immediately (even though it has been a nuisance). We only had to do that a couple of times for each child to stop bad behaviour dead in its tracks. So, word up your friends and family that you are experiencing behavioural problems and that you may have to unexpectedly bundle everything up and go home. That way if an episode occurs, you'll have them on your side and supporting you rather than undermining you.'

Amanda

Bad habits

Your tot is intrigued. He has discovered his nostrils and his penis – with gusto! You are feeling grossed out by the nose-picking, and playing with his 'willy' in public is enough to make you pretend you don't know him (if only he'd stop calling you Mummy!). But whether your child is a boy or girl, bodily parts are a sensory experience – nose holes, vaginas and penises are fascinating places with interesting feelings and textures. For some kids, fiddling with their 'bits' can be a bit of a boredom buster; for others it is a form of self-soothing, and can just as easily turn to habit.

Even though you may be squirming and just want to shout, 'Stop that, right now!' it can help to chill out. Drawing attention to socially inappropriate behaviour is more likely to prolong it (not only does it feel good but I have Mummy taking lots of notice of me, too!). So, as you breathe deeply and slowly (to help you calm down), ask yourself, what is the worst that can happen, apart from being embarrassed and feeling like puking (you, that is)? Eating boogers won't actually make your tot sick, although picking the sensitive membranes in his nostrils might, and while the grime in the bathwater probably won't hurt either, a good dose of soap bubbles could give him a bit of diarrhoea, and no matter how much he fiddles, his penis won't drop off either.

'I think masturbation is normal in little boys so I tend to ignore it, although I did draw the line at my son pulling it out for a play at a cafe once. With my daughter I haven't experienced that yet. As for boogers, each to their own. I figure they will probably grow out of it. I have been offered many and told they are delicious, but I must decline!'

Kelli

So how do you get a toddler to modify his exploration of his body? Distraction and diversion are your best weapons: keep your child's hands occupied – pass him a toy or book or try a finger game like 'incy wincy spider' or 'wheels on the bus'. If singing and waving your arms around in public is almost as embarrassing as your tot's behaviour, simply hold his hand and engage him in conversation as you keep him busy helping you choose the groceries or give him an alternative object to fiddle with. If his nose is the prime target, pass him a tissue each time you see a finger heading that way.

'We have always found that when we react to so-called "bad behaviour" with simple diversions and nurturing, we actually get the message through much easier and quicker. For example, if our daughter picks her nose, we offer her a tissue. Most times she will take the tissue as if we are giving her some help, yet if we told her it is yucky to pick her nose and she must use a tissue she would fight us over it and pick it more. If our daughter is clingy, we find that giving her extra cuddles means that she will go off on her own to play quicker and happier.'

Linda

Try to work out if there is a reason behind bad habits:

❀ Is your toddler bored? Engage him in activities rather than plonking him in front of television where idle hands will find their own 'work'.

❀ Is he meeting a need for sensory stimulation to help his little nervous system develop? (See Sensory play, page 134, for ideas to provide alternative and more socially acceptable sensory stimulation.)

❀ Does your child have allergies that make his nose itchy? Usually a child with allergies will push his nose upwards in an 'allergic salute' rather than pick it, but he could have dry, itchy nasal membranes, especially if he has recently had a cold. You can reduce itching by keeping his nostrils moist: pop a bit of natural baby barrier balm (be careful not to use a cream that could irritate his sensitive skin further) around the outside of his nostrils and use saline nose drops during the day and a vaporiser at night.

✿ If he drinks bathwater, could your little one simply be thirsty? Try offering fresh water in a plastic cup and keep him busy playing with bath toys to distract him from drinking the bubbles. By the time he is three, showing him the scum around the bath will probably gross him out enough to put him off.

'Normal child behaviour – like playing with their body parts and picking their nose – doesn't worry me. I explain you don't do it in public, and your bottom carries bacteria which can make you sick. My son is a typical boy who plays with his penis constantly. At the start of school this year, I told him that if I saw him holding his penis, I'd say, "Hands on head!" and he'd know to let go. I explained he'd get teased if he did it at school.'

Bronni

Beyond bad behaviour

If you suspect your child may have behaviour problems that may require special help – from food allergies to sensory motor problems or a more serious disorder like Asperger's syndrome (a type of autism) or attention deficit disorder – it is wise to contact an early childhood professional such as your child health nurse, your child's preschool teacher or paediatrician.

If your child does have a disorder that requires intervention, it is best to get help as early as possible. (See the Resources section for some helpful websites.) If his challenging behaviour is simply due to immature development, you will at least be reassured and can seek guidance on how best to support and guide him.

'Before our daughter was diagnosed with Selective Mutism at three years of age, we couldn't understand why she would never say please or thank you. She couldn't even manage yes or no when she was being offered sweets from a restaurant waiter or anyone else like that. "She's just shy," we'd awkwardly respond. The thing was that it seemed she was super shy from birth and we were eagerly waiting for her to grow out of it. It was frustrating for me because I felt judged as a parent, that I hadn't taught her manners well, when in fact she was

fabulous with them at home. But we just had no idea of the abnormally high levels of anxiety the situation created to make her "shut off" when people spoke to her. Like a fear of heights, she feared being heard. She barely spoke in three-year-old kinder and, unfortunately, she didn't have a very understanding teacher which made it a tough year.

'People who know nothing about SM think children like this are manipulative. Some people saw it as a challenge to make her talk, which only made it worse. Things have improved through psychology sessions, though the first vocalisations she made were noises and actions – silly behaviour – which is a natural progression of SM. Dealing with that behaviour made it even harder to cope with my daughter's illness, especially as I also had another toddler son. On top of that, even some of my own family told me her behaviour was the result of us raising her to be independent, which was not the problem at all. We have boundaries and rules and she knows I mean it when I say that I will take those scissors off her if she cuts her hair and not the paper. It's been an incredibly isolating and anxiety-ridden time for us all – but by far the most difficult thing has been dealing with people's perceptions and misunderstanding.'

Kelly

Mummy meltdowns

We all have our ideals of the good parent, the good child (who is often good because of the exemplary efforts of his good parents) and the good family. The truth is that there will often be discrepancies between our ideal images (and certainly the media images), and our reality. Many times, we lack the resources (sleep, support, time, money, sleep, inspiration, creativity, wisdom, sleep and a sense of humour) to live up to any image that even resembles 'good enough', let alone ideal.

'After the birth of my second baby, a lot of things changed. All of a sudden I couldn't instantly respond to my first child as I had before, because I had a new baby to attend to. I was unable to nap during the day as I had with my first baby, so I was more affected by sleep deprivation than ever before. For the first time I started losing my temper with my first child.

'At times I found it overwhelming to deal with a newborn baby plus the demands of my energetic three-year-old. It was as if there was a monster lurking within me, ready to lash out in a split second. I simply did not have the capacity to respond to my eldest daughter in the way she was used to. There were times when all I wanted to do was indulge in my new baby

without interruptions and I started snapping at my first daughter in frustration. It felt like the foundations I had built with her were crumbling.

'It took a lot of conscious effort on my part to make sure I was keeping the loving connection with my toddler, and including her in the care of our new baby. I think sleep deprivation was a major cause of my angry outbursts. After a few months, things started to settle. I found it really valuable to be able to spend some quality time exclusively with my older child when the baby was sleeping, and let some of the household tasks go for a bit. It was also really good to get out and visit friends so my three-year-old could play with some children her own age. This helped her to enjoy being a bit more "grown up" rather than wanting to be a baby again.

'When our little one started walking things shifted again, and the two of them started playing together. The youngest still needs a lot of attention and I continue to remind myself to reach out and cuddle my first child, who is now four. Almost eighteen months later we can't imagine what life would be like without the two of them. They are gorgeous together and play beautifully, but those first few months were really challenging.'

Alice

When we feel pushed to the limit, our children can seem to be out to get us. As they push all of our buttons at once and catapult us into our out-of-control zone, we react in ways that are irrational and out of proportion. We open our mouths to teach our child a lesson and out comes – our mother! Not only are we the parent we don't want to be, we have turned into the parent we swore we would never become.

This road rage of parenting can happen to the best of us. And just as road rage isn't usually about the road, our reaction when our kids wind us up is often about something much deeper than simple annoyance or concern for their wellbeing (as we may justify). In fact, it's more likely to be about our need for order and control than their need for understanding and connection.

When we shout and snap, or say things we regret, we go on 'automatic'. Daniel Goleman, author of *Emotional Intelligence*, refers to automatics as 'emotional hijacking', describing our normally rational mind as being taken over by emotions. Automatics are our attempt to control our child's behaviour in order for us to feel better and for them to react differently. Yet, when we allow our kids to wind us up, our attempts to control the situation become futile – we lose authority, break connection, and both of us can end up feeling angry, defensive, frightened and inadequate, so nothing productive can be learned.

It's a normal biological reaction to yell if we feel threatened, and sometimes we can't avoid yelling if we see a threat to our child's safety, but there is always value in thinking if things could have been done differently. Even when the button-pushing seems deliberate, it is important to ask, what is happening here? It may be an effort by your child to connect with a busy or distracted parent (you!), regardless of the reaction it will elicit, or it could be that a child is having difficulty expressing feelings, and physical factors like tiredness or hunger can also play a part. Remember, too, that you are a role-model for your child, and you are teaching how to (or how not to) handle stress.

'I think when we have those meltdowns it is the final warning our body is giving us that we have become bankrupt. At that point we better put in some deposits as no more withdrawals are coming out unless they are nasty letters of demand! When I get to that point, I demand John stay home for the day or come home early, because I know I will only do more damage to the kids – I hate them having a screaming banshee mummy.'

Kelly

Staying calm and in charge

❀ **Know your limits.** As soon as you feel yourself becoming wound up, take a deep breath and step back. You won't be able to do anything effective if you explode.

❀ **Look behind the behaviour.** Remind yourself that your child is *having* a problem, not *being* a problem. Try to work out what is behind the behaviour, even if the provoking seems deliberate.

❀ **Accentuate the positive.** Try to remember that your child's irritating characteristics – sensitivity, persistence and initiative – will be valued when he's six feet tall! When you are really having trouble liking your child (yes, this is normal some days), remind yourself that you have a fabulous little person in your family and that you aren't a bad parent who is growing a monster.

Try to get back on track by making a simple chart: draw a sun (a circle with rays, just as your child might draw) on a large sheet of paper, decorate it with glue and glitter or stars and crayons, and inside the circle, write your child's name. On the rays you can write lovely things about your child (yes, there will be some, really!). Stop and think what you like about your child, what you enjoy or what he is doing that is positive and write these things on each sun ray. Try turning annoyances into positives. For instance: poking toast into the dog's mouth is sharing; dressing herself, no matter how wackily, is independence; and climbing is developing motor skills.

Leave some rays blank to fill in later. Now, pop your chart on a wall or the fridge, and when you find yourself enjoying a moment with your child, write this on your chart – it may be as simple as 'laughing' (don't berate yourself for not being elaborate, this isn't supposed to add to your stress). Soon you will see that even though his behaviour can be trying, your child really is a lovely little being (at least, some of the time). By shifting your own attitude and appreciating the interesting little character you have, things will start to go along more smoothly as you connect with your child and he responds to your positive energy.

✿ **Nurture *you*.** When your own stress levels are high, a child's inconvenient behaviour (scattered toys, a spilt drink) can be the proverbial straw that breaks the camel's back, so be kind to yourself. Prioritise, and learn to say no to demands and people that drain your energy. Think of things you can do to nurture *you* and make a list to keep in a prominent place as a reminder for when you have a few minutes to yourself. Your list might include things like painting your toenails, brushing your hair, playing some music other than nursery rhymes, burning some nice oils, taking a walk in the park with your tot (cabin fever is a downer for mum and child) and breathing deeply. Or, after the little rascals are in bed, instead of racing to catch-up on chores, take a bubble bath – alone! Also, think of ways to work in with friends: invite another mum over so you can watch the kids (and groan and laugh) together, or start a babysitting club among your mums' group so you can all take turns at having some respite.

'I love my garden, so in the early days with baby number two, I would put him in a pram to watch me work for a while and when he got sick of that, he would get tied onto my back and would eventually go to sleep. It meant that I got a little time in my own head, doing something that I really enjoy.

'I try to get time to have an uninterrupted cup of tea in the morning. It sounds like such a small thing but it means a great deal to me and, most days, it is achievable. It means that I am not disappointed at the end of the day when I don't have "me" time.'

Mandy

'The best nurturing technique for me was to put both kids in family daycare for a day a week. For them it was a chance to play with new toys with another child or two. It wasn't as overwhelming as a big daycare centre; both kids were always together, and there were only four kids to the motherly adult looking after them. On those days, I never did any housework or cooking, let the answering machine take messages, and did whatever I wanted to do for myself.'

Sonia

Toddler tactic: share the load

It can be hard to find space for yourself with a toddler under-foot. It can also be tedious trying to amuse a single child and get tasks done. So why not relieve the stress of isolation and the frustration by sharing children and your workload with another mum or two? Take turns going to each other's homes and having a 'cook-up', a clean-up or a working bee in the garden. With luck and good planning (you can designate one mum to watch the kids while two tackle the tasks), the children will amuse each other for short bursts while you get some work done.

Chapter five
Play and learning

You didn't get around to making baby flashcards, you didn't have a curriculum beyond cuddles when he was a three-month-old, and now your toddler would rather make mud pies than do maths. Are you feeling guilty that you might be depriving your child?

If your toddler resists being buckled into his car seat and rushed off to one more class because he would rather 'just play', relax, he won't miss out on achieving his potential. Play, to the toddler, is his work. Your child is 'at work' (and learning) all day, every day: the spirit of a child's work as he constructs a cubby, makes a production line of mud pies or creates a masterpiece with finger paints, isn't much different from the spirit of a scientist's laboratory, a chef's kitchen, an artist's studio or an architect's office.

'My kids would much prefer to play with "real" stuff rather than toys. They play with Tupperware or plastics, sardine tins, small unopened boxes of food and packets of pasta. My three-year-

old loves to "help" more than play with her toys. I give her small but very important jobs to do while I'm cooking or cleaning. For the times when I'm busy and don't really want any help, I tell her this and get down a hidden box of toys or puzzles that will keep her interest.

'We have a few music CDs that are great for using up energy. I join in from time to time and teach the kids some dance moves. They will often dance by themselves for ages. Messy outside activities are also really appreciated by my kids. All-over body painting (on naked bodies in the shade) is a favourite as are mud pies, a bath of uncooked lentils and rice, or just playing in the dirt with a bucket of water. Games of hide and seek or shopkeeper with Mum (usually while I'm folding washing, putting it away or tidying up) are a great way to give them attention but still get things done. Mostly the kids just love being where I am and will happily amuse themselves with whatever is in that room or space. When I'm exhausted or ill, a game of "draw on Mum's legs with a pen while she watches TV" goes down really well.'

Sonia

Through play, your child is making sense of the world around him: he is learning to get along with others, solve problems and handle stressful situations. He is also developing perceptual motor skills, strength, balance and coordination as he learns to differentiate sizes and shapes, concentrate, listen to others, learn rules, express ideas and cooperate with playmates. Play also encourages creativity and language skills as your child uses his imagination, discovers his feelings and learns how other people feel – this is a sound base for emotional intelligence.

It is these skills learnt incidentally, as your child plays, that will form a strong foundation for later learning, not hours spent teaching him to write his name or sound-out letters. In fact, reading and writing will probably happen more easily if your child has spent many happy hours 'just playing'. Forcing your child into early intellectual learning, rather than allowing him to get on with his own 'work' of creatively playing, may cause him to miss out on vital skills needed for later learning, to become disenchanted and discouraged from formal learning.

Making playtime fun doesn't involve lots of structured activities or expensive equipment, but it does require respect from you for your child's 'work'. This means that rather than directing or taking over your child's play, it is better to be present and observe carefully, taking your cues from your child: if he is sitting quietly, sit quietly with him; if he is boisterous and active, join in his game and follow his rules, with gentle guidance only to ensure safety. This will help him feel competent and valued and will encourage him to develop initiative and perseverance.

Toddler tactic: respect play

✿ *Remember, your child's fantasy world is his own: you can nurture and encourage but be careful not to impose adult values.*

✿ *Switch off the television while your child is playing: play means active involvement, not passive distraction.*

✿ *Alternate quiet and active play periods.*

✿ *If you aren't in the mood, don't initiate a game because you feel you should. Your toddler will sense your reluctance and you will probably both become frustrated.*

✿ *Don't race around tidying everything behind your child. Try to have a play area where things can be left out so your tot can pick up his 'work' where he left off.*

✿ *Give children a few minutes' warning that it's nearly time to stop playing, rather than insisting they pack up now! Imagine how you would feel if you were busily working at a task and somebody ordered you to stop immediately!*

✿ *Remember, play is fun. It is the process (what your toddler enjoys) that counts, not the product (what he or she can do).*

How children play

Unless you have more than one child, you will be chief play-mate and teacher. Even if you have several children, unless there is an age gap of a few years, playing together peaceably without supervision will be a challenge for a while yet. While toddlers love the company of other children, and playgroups are fun (especially for parents who need reassurance that their child's spirited behaviour is actually on track), the ability to share toys and play cooperatively will take time and depends on stages of maturity.

One-year-olds often wander around by themselves, exploring and occasionally taking a toy from another child or imitating their actions, but generally they don't really play with other children. This kind of play is called 'solitary play' by the experts.

Between **two-and-a-half** and three, little ones begin to engage in 'parallel play', which means that two children may play alongside each other but without much interaction – they might both play with cars or build with blocks but they will be playing separately.

When they are closer to **three years old**, toddlers begin to play cooperatively, perhaps building a road together in the sandpit or making a block tower. Developmental readiness to play together varies a fair bit and can be gender related: girls may be able to play cooperatively at two-and-a-half while boys are closer to four when this happens, and sharing treasured toys and attention (especially their parents') can take a while yet.

So please don't give up on playgroups or play dates because it seems like a waste of time. Despite his developmental stage right now, with your support, your child will gradually learn to get along with other children and adults, and will enjoy meeting people in a familiar setting. By making this commitment, you are sowing seeds for the development of later social skills such as sharing, empathy, fairness and self-control.

'My children love playing together. Even the baby joins in and crawls around after them. They dress up and put on dance routines. They also do learning activities together. Many of their books are ones they can use to learn in a fun way (with puzzles and so on). They have a wide variety of toys – I try to give them toys that will help them develop skills such as throwing and catching.'

Bronni

The toy box

Aren't toyshops overwhelming? It can be tempting to grab all the exciting and fabulous toys you see, especially when they come with a promise to make your child smarter or enhance his skills. Then there are the friends and relatives who can't resist buying toys. Often though, your child is just as interested in the packaging as what's in the box.

As well as working out which toys are appropriate to your child's stage of development, you will find 'less is more' is a good adage when offering toys to play with. It is better to present a few toys or a small basket of things at a time. Instead of having all the toys constantly available, it is better to rotate them – bring out one or two toys at a time, then put those away and swap over to different ones. This way, your child will be able to concentrate and play, rather than simply dragging toys out and scattering them around. It is also a good idea to try toys from a toy library, especially if you are considering buying more expensive items and you are unsure whether they will be a delight or just become unused clutter.

'I have three large boxes filled with toys and books. I rotate them on a fortnightly basis or so. This refreshes my children's

interest in toys as well as keeping the clutter out of their bed-room. We also have the "Boring Box" which is full of activities and forgotten toys that come out when boredom strikes or I am on the phone for a long time.'

Sonia

Storage is an important consideration. A jumble of mixed-up toys is confusing and overwhelming to a child but if you sort and store toys carefully, your child can find them easily and pack them away afterwards (with your help). As well as toy boxes or baskets, drawstring bags are handy for keeping games and puzzles together.

Whether he is young enough to need you to engage in his play or whether your child is happy to entertain himself, he will play more contentedly if his play space is near you. That's right – forget the home beautifying, and bring on the kiddy-sized furniture. In fact, a child-sized table can be invaluable for little people: when our children were small I had an old school table and chairs in the family room. This was great for activities such as playdough or pasting as well as meals during the day. Also, as I am not a morning person, I found it helpful to set up an activity at the table before I went to bed each night (playdough and cutters, blocks with little people or cars, a box of dress-up hats and a mirror, or clay with feathers, sticks and shells). This way, as I got started in the morning on breakfast and chores, the children could play without being under my still-snoozy feet.

You can also encourage happy play by setting up several play stations (no, not the electronic kind!). Delegate specific areas for different types of play such as a quiet games or reading corner with some comfy cushions or a beanbag; a dress-up corner with a clothes tree and a few costumes hanging on it; a cooking corner with a toy stove (an empty box will do fine) and a few old bowls and spoons, for instance.

When you are choosing toys, it is better to have a few quality toys that will engage your child and be useful for a while, rather than a whole stack of two-minute wonders that will be tossed aside as he loses interest. It is also sensible (and environmentally responsible) to consider how many plastic toys you provide for your toddler and how many of these are very much the same from a sensory perspective. Plastic feels, smells and tastes the same whatever its shape, so include some other textures in your child's toy box. Natural objects such as wooden blocks, pine cones and soft dolls made from cloth or felt can encourage imaginary play and will far outlast an expensive, single-function plastic toy with a few shiny buttons to push.

'When we chopped down our plum tree, we cut a stack of circles from a small branch and sanded the edges smooth (but left the 'roughish' bark on the outside of the circles) to make wooden blocks. Our one-year-old loves to stack these and they can also be used creatively as "cakes" or "money" or whatever else older children like to imagine in their games.'

Larissa

'Some of our plastic toys only come out when other kids come over to play. Three-year-old Euan's favourite toys are the dinosaurs we've collected. He's dinosaur mad and knows them all, often correcting me when I mistake a pterodactyl for an anhanguera.

'We spend a lot of our time outdoors so Euan has a set of garden tools (spades, rakes, hoes) that he helps out with in the vegetable patch. We look for ants, mites, bees, butterflies and birds in the garden, and then chat about whatever we find.

'We have loads of books and there's usually at least one time during the day when we will read three or four stories together.'

Mandy

As well as your basic toy box you can create a variety of other, smaller boxes that can be brought out at special times or on rainy days to encourage play as your tot grows bigger and seems to need extra stimulation.

Dress-up box

Little ones love dressing up, sometimes as part of a game and sometimes just to wear a costume as they play.

❀ Collect a selection of hats then let your little one try them on and look at himself in a mirror.

❀ Pull-on skirts and trousers with elastic waists, capes of different fabrics and simple velcro fasteners make it easier for toddlers to dress themselves.

❀ Second-hand shops and fetes are real treasure troves of exciting dress-ups. Shorten the hems on evening dresses so your child doesn't trip over them and look out for waistcoats, sparkly shoes, feather boas, fabulous handbags, jewellery (for older toddlers) and anything with sequins or frills.

❀ If you sew, brightly coloured lycra or stretchy jersey or fleece fabrics are good for costumes as they don't need hemming – just cut (into pointy hats, circular skirts or tunics), sew the side seams, add elastic for skirts and trousers and voila!

Useful box

A useful box can be filled with craft materials for collage, construction or an emergency costume. (It is amazing what a desperate, sleep-deprived mother can make from old pantyhose, wire coat-hangers and a roll of cooking foil.)

❀ Collect empty containers, boxes and cardboard tubes that can be glued together. If your child has allergies or is likely to play with children with allergies (check with their parents before you drag out the useful box) you may have to forgo egg cartons or cereal boxes.

❀ Include fabric scraps, bits of leather or wool (lamb's wool as well as yarn), used wrapping paper, lids, bubble wrap, stickers and stars – in fact, anything that you would usually throw out that can be glued or taped to make masks, dolls' furniture, a cardboard city, or simply cut up for practice using scissors.

❀ Also include natural materials such as seed pods, bark, feathers and shells for creative play.

Music box

Simple, homemade musical instruments or store-bought instruments can be stored together where they can be easily found when you want to strike up the band.

❁ Include tambourines, maracas, a drum or two, xylo-phones, shakers (small, egg-shaped shakers are great for little hands) and bells (either on elastic to wear around wrists or ankles or securely attached to a handle to shake).

❁ You can make your own shakers by filling small jars with different grains then gluing lids on tightly.

Choosing toys for toddlers

To choose toys appropriately, it is important to be guided by the ages listed on the packaging. Despite having a child who is 'terribly advanced for his age', your toddler is likely to be at risk of choking on toys with small parts and this may be one reason a toy is labelled as suitable for children over three years. Here is a guide for choosing age-appropriate toys.

One- to two-year-olds

❁ Action toys – toys that can be moved or make noises according to the child's actions – such as hammer and pegs, spinning tops, jack-in-the-boxes and push-button toys that make sounds or flash lights.

❁ Toys that encourage large muscle activity. Try tunnels to

crawl through, low ladders and slides to climb on, toys on wheels, ride-ons and rockers, and toys that can be filled, emptied and dumped such as trucks and trolleys.

✿ Toys that encourage manipulative skills, problem-solving and eye–hand coordination such as lids, switches, dials, knobs, stacking and nesting toys, shape sorters, blocks and simple puzzles.

✿ Balls – soft balls, textured balls, balls that make noises, even balls from the pet shop with bells inside.

✿ Bath toys. These can be shop-bought toys or simple household containers that can be filled, emptied and poured from.

✿ Musical instruments – shakers, triangles, xylophones, drums, maracas.

✿ Books – choose books and stories with repetition, picture books, nursery rhyme books, tactile books and peekaboo books.

✿ Social toys such as dolls, stuffed toys, simple dress-ups such as hats, kitchen things (to pretend cook), a small table and chairs.

Two- to three-year-olds

✿ Props for imaginary play such as dress-ups, little people, cars and tools such as toy lawnmowers, wheelbarrows, watering cans, rakes, brooms and other child-sized tools. You could make a kitchen from a small table or wooden box with painted hotplates.

✿ Construction play. Try building blocks and interlocking blocks.

✿ Toys that encourage gross motor skills and active play such as tunnels, trikes, scooters, climbing structures, stationary outdoor equipment (swings, slides and trampolines, used with safety nets and careful supervision) and balls of all sizes.

✿ Toys to encourage fine motor skills such as blocks, interlocking rings, nuts and bolts, puzzles, cylinders that require screwing together, peg boards (with larger pieces to prevent choking) and picture dominoes.

✿ Toys to encourage creative and artistic play. Try chalk and a blackboard, crayons (these are a better sensory experience than felt-tipped pens and easier to clean up), playdough and finger paints. Also consider an Etch A Sketch – a toy that allows you to draw then wipe clean pictures. This is a good toy for travelling or to amuse a toddler while you feed the baby.

What about violent toys?

On the topic of violent toys, the research is reassuring. According to Dr Kathleen Alfano, psychologist and director of the Fisher Price Research Department in the United States, 'research shows that the toy is neutral; it's what a child takes to play that matters, so it's important that parents understand what trauma the child is exposed to. If a child is trying to work through something traumatic while playing, it should be talked about.'

It is wise to monitor television, even children's programs that can be scary or provide violent role-models for little ones. It is also important that you don't allow children to act violently towards another person. However, according to Jeffrey Goldstein, professor of Media and Communication at the University of Utrecht in the Netherlands, aggressive play does have some positive elements. In his book *Toys, Play and Child Development*, Professor Goldstein says, 'aggressive play requires cooperation and helps a child learn limits and self-control. There is a clear distinction between aggressive play and aggressive behaviour and children instinctively know the difference.'

'We refused to buy guns for our children, but for our three-year-old son, every stick became a gun or a sword. We had piles of sticks collected from every walk we went on. We thought it was better not to make a fuss other than to insist that swords and guns stayed outside, and he was really very imaginative. His play wasn't violent towards other children, he just used to tuck a stick into the side of his trousers as his sword and off he would go, like a little man on a mission, hunting for bears or tigers. Later, he just grew out of this phase.'

Ally

Aggressive play also allows children to release their boundless energy. This applies especially to boys who need to find positive ways to use it up in non-destructive ways. Professor Goldstein says, 'I would be concerned about aggressive play if it was an obsession but if it is part of a range of play, I'd consider it a normal part of boyhood.'

Toddler tactic: try cuddles instead of bullets!

Introduce the idea of cuddle guns. Teach your child that instead of bullets, his imaginary guns fire cuddles. If he shoots a playmate, he has to give a cuddle – wow! There are cuddles all around.

Imaginative play

To your child, his imaginary world is real. You may feel tempted to tell your little one that fairies are 'just pretend' or that dinosaurs don't exist but this can dampen his flow of ideas and halt fantasy play, which helps your child to work through real-life situations and feel in control of his ever-expanding world. Imaginative play helps your child develop initiative and confidence. Through role play, especially, your child is processing her own experiences as she bakes a pretend cake, puts the baby to bed or drives off to work in her Tonka truck.

You can nurture your child's imagination by providing simple things to play with rather than sophisticated 'finished' toys. For instance, in the dress-up box, include pieces of beautiful fabric and scarves as well as clothing, since fabric can become capes and robes according to how children like to wrap and tie them. Also provide a basket of old sheets or bedspreads and large pieces of stronger fabric and clip-on clothes pegs so children can improvise – they may use cloth to make cubbies, sails for a ship or a circus tent.

Also, don't be surprised or intervene if you notice your child using toys for purposes other than their original use – a doll's pram could be a cowboy's wagon, toy boxes may be upturned and emptied to make a train, a brick can become a delicious cake, a bowl of mud can become dinner and (despite your most gentle parenting efforts and discouragement of violent play) sticks can become brilliant guns or swords. (See Everyday magic, page 171.)

Sensory play

Children absorb the world through all of their senses: hearing, sight, smell, touch and taste. Touch is the first sense to develop and your child's body (just like your own) is covered with very sensitive touch receptors. Through these he will receive information about hot and cold, hard and soft, smooth and rough, what hurts and what feels good. When his sense of touch is working properly, messages to your child's brain will see him touching appropriately – he will quickly take his hand off a hot heater and he might (just maybe!) keep a jumper on if it is really cold.

You can encourage the development of your little one's immature nervous system through tactile experiences as well as movement. Stimulation of your child's senses encourages neural connections in your toddler's rapidly developing brain, and this will help with sensory perception which allows your child to make sense of his world – literally!

For the first couple of years, all you need to do is provide lots of cuddles and love, and your child will soak up the natural sensory experiences of his environment. These include: skin-to-skin contact as you feed, cuddle and massage him; the feeling of fabric against his skin or your own clothing as you hold him; movement as you carry and rock him, bounce him on your knee, dance with him or push him in a stroller or on the swings at the park; tastes as he tries different foods; cooking smells (freshly brewed coffee, warm bread), as well as smells such as freshly mown grass, wet leaves, flowers or herbs in the garden; and interesting noises like birds singing, wind chimes, insects buzzing, cars tooting, music or people chattering and singing.

You can also plan activities that provide lots of sensory play, from listening games (get him to close his eyes and guess the noise as you ring a bell, munch an apple, pour water or scrunch paper) to activities that involve smelling, feeling and tasting. For some fun sensory play, roll up your sleeves, and try some of these ideas:

✿ **Make a magic scarf box.** Is your one-year-old crazy about pulling tissues out of packets? Try providing this alternative sensory experience. Collect colourful scarves or squares of different soft fabrics. Knot them together at one corner to make a long trail. Now put your trail of scarves into an empty ice-cream container. Make a hole and knot the last scarf to the lid, then make a hole in the bottom of the container to pull the scarves through (the bottom of the container will become the top of your magic scarf box). Put the lid on the container, with the scarves squashed loosely inside. Pull the tip of the first scarf through the hole and show your little one how to pull the scarf through to reveal the next brightly coloured silky scarf, and the next . . .

✿ **Pizza massage.** Massage is a lovely way to stay 'in touch' with your child. It also helps develop your child's nervous system. Here is a game that will encourage even the most active toddler to stay (fairly) still as you massage.

Offer to make a massage 'pizza' on your child's back. Get your little one to help choose 'ingredients', and as you add each ingredient, alter your massage strokes to represent the ingredient. For instance:

'Roll' out the dough, using long firm strokes with your palms across the child's back, moving from side to side, making smaller circles to get the dough 'into the corners'.

'Spread' tomato paste, using smooth strokes.

'Chop' vegetables, making a chopping motion with the sides of your hands.

'Sprinkle' cheese with gentle finger taps.

Let your imagination (and your child's) run wild.

Happy 'cooking'!

❀ **A touchy feely pool.** For a wonderful sensory experience, fill plastic sand-pit shells (also called 'clams') with various non-messy materials: different-sized and textured balls, Styrofoam pieces, packing material, paper, cellophane, different textured fabrics, foam sponges. Then let your children climb right in. They can really 'immerse' themselves in fun!

Or part-fill a large plastic dish or baby bath with rice and give your child funnels and cups to pour and mix as he feels the rice (this is best done outside since rice tramples a long distance!).

❀ **Hacky sacks.** Balloons (not blown up) filled with any mix of textured dry goods become coloured hacky sacks for feeling, squishing, guessing, matching, throwing and catching. Use rice, beans, peas, lentils, flour or water and cover each filled balloon by stretching several layers of different coloured balloons over the top to protect from bursting and spillage.

❀ **Playdough.** This can soothe your child as he squishes and squeezes, or ease frustration as he kneads and punches, and it is a creative medium with endless possibilities.

It doesn't matter whether your child simply pokes and squeezes, or tears pieces of dough at first. As well as encouraging your little one to squish the dough with her fingers, you can provide tools such as a blunt or plastic knife, a fork, a plastic melon ball shaper or a garlic press. She'll enjoy watching the long wriggly strands as she squeezes playdough through the holes of the garlic press. As your child's imagination and vocabulary develop, add birthday candles, toothpicks and other decorations for her 'cakes', and encourage your child to make animals and creatures as well. She can also make boats (with toothpicks and paper sails), or scenery such as caves, bridges and mountains. Add some of your child's play figures and help her make up her own games (the little people can live in the cave or climb the mountains).

Playdough recipe

You'll need:

   2 cups plain flour

   1 cup salt

   2 tablespoons oil

4 teaspoons cream of tartar

food colouring

2 cups water

Combine the flour, salt, oil, cream of tartar and food colouring of your choice. Add the water a little at a time, mixing everything together. Cook over a low heat for about five minutes, stirring all the time. When the mixture leaves the side of the saucepan, it's ready. Cool the dough to a comfortable temperature, then create! This mixture keeps well in an airtight container.

For an extra stimulating sensory experience, add essences with strong smells such as lemon, mint, almond, vanilla or orange. You could also colour the dough to match its smell (yellow and lemon, green with mint, orange smell and colour).

❀ **Slime.** A soothing treat best enjoyed outdoors. As a wonderful, gooey, tactile experience, forgo artistic aspirations and plonk the slime into a baby bath, add funnels and cups and let your toddler pour, squeeze, squelch and ooze!

Slime recipe

1 cup Lux soap flakes

3 cups hot water

powder paint or food colouring

> Mix the soap flakes and hot water. Stir vigorously until the soap
> has dissolved, then leave the mixture to set overnight. Slime
> can be whipped with an eggbeater and powder paint or food
> colouring to make finger paint.

❀ **Finger paint.** If you aren't in the mood for mess, leave
this until another day – or try it outside. Use newspaper,
butcher's paper or paint directly on a tabletop. To save
table-top artworks, press a sheet of paper onto the artwork then hang it up to dry and be admired.

Finger paint recipe

> 1 cup cornflour
> 2 tablespoons sugar
> 3 cups cold water
> food colouring
>
> In a saucepan, mix the cornflour and sugar together then add
> the cold water. Stir over a low heat until the mixture is well
> blended. Divide the mixture into three or four parts and add a
> different food colour to each.

❀ **Shaving cream finger paint.** Here's a short-cut: squeeze
a tube of shaving cream on the kitchen table or (if your
table is lovely polished wood) a play table and let your

child delight in finger painting with this easy-to-clean-up option. You can add a few sprinkles of powder paint to sustain his interest and if the shaving cream becomes dry, just add a few drops of water or more shaving cream. When your toddler has finished painting, simply rinse his hands and dry them. The shaving cream paint can be wiped off the table with a paper towel. Even though a little lick is harmless, this is more appropriate for children over two when they are less likely to taste test their creations.

Creative play

Paint, paper, glue, scissors and lots of mess are all part of your child's early experiences in learning to plan and organise. Artistic creativity is an expression of your toddler's ideas and feelings, so, rather than balk at the potential mayhem, why not support and enjoy your budding Picasso?

Just like most other stages of development, your child's drawings and paintings will follow a natural sequence that is universal among small children. At **eighteen months** your toddler is probably a 'disordered scribbler', which means that in this phase he will use whole arm movements to draw. His first attempts at creative expression will be lines that are random and uncontrolled.

At about **two years old** your little artist will reach the 'controlled scribble' stage. Now your toddler's coordination and control allow her to make more deliberate lines which generally go up and down and back and forth, and she will be starting to make connections in her mind with what she is doing. Soon she will be doing circular scribbling.

By about **three years of age**, he will be able to draw a circle. About now, he will enter the 'named scribbling' stage. Although he may not have any idea what he intends to draw, he will name his creation after he has completed it. With a little more development in this phase, your toddler may think of what he wants to draw before he puts crayons to paper. Although you may not be able to see a big truck in your little fellow's picture, to him, it will look just like a big truck!

Toddler tactic: give him a mirror

At about three, your toddler will draw his first face. His initial attempts will be oddly shaped and the features will not be in the right place, but if you give him a mirror to look into as he draws, this will help him to draw a face with details such as eyelashes and eyebrows as well as facial features that look more balanced.

To nurture your toddler's creative spirit and encourage him to express his ideas and feelings through art:

. ❀ Use good materials and tools. Also, be aware of the endless variety of natural materials that can be used artistically such as plants, shells and seeds.
❀ Offer only one or two materials or paint colours at a time, so that your child is not overwhelmed.
❀ Be prepared before beginning a project. Have the workspace and materials ready so you can focus on your little one or you could find yourself as frustrated as your child if he makes a mess when you are distracted (even for a moment) by trying to find art materials.
❀ Gently guide your child on the use of materials but don't correct or add to his artwork. 'Hands off!' is a good rule.
❀ Allow plenty of time. Remember, your child learns from doing. The process is important, rather than the finished product.
❀ Be respectful. Show the attitude that everybody's artwork is special, important and beautiful. Encourage your child to explore, experiment and express his own ideas and feelings. And remember, how you talk to your child about his art will influence his creativity.

Rather than trying to guess what your child has drawn or asking him, 'What is that?', ask him to tell you about his picture. If he can't because he doesn't really know what it is, you can comment on something specific such as, 'I like those long red lines!', 'You must have drawn really fast to make those big circles!' or 'What a lovely soft blue line!' As you talk, point to the parts of the picture you are describing. As well as making your little one feel special and important, you will be extending his language and helping him learn colours and shapes.

❀ Display your child's beautiful artwork. Hang some pictures at her eye level and, as her collection starts to take over the house, send some to Grandma to admire and hang up. A framed drawing makes a very special gift and says to your child, 'We value your work.'

Exploring the natural world

Little children are fascinated by nature: they love to shake seed pods, romp in autumn leaves, walk barefoot in soft grass, jump in rain puddles and squish in mud. To little ones there is magic in the sun rising and setting, wind blowing, rain washing down the windows and flowers opening in spring. By nurturing this wonder, we are helping our children's spirituality develop and teaching them to respect and care for the earth.

Toddlers don't need scientific explanations about global warming or to be made fearful about the folly of wasting resources. Instead, we can share their wonder by talking in a language that is meaningful to them: 'Look! Jack Frost has painted the windows with ice,' or 'Please don't walk on the new grass, you might squash the seed babies.' By watching adults they love model gestures like recycling water or rubbish (with your child's help), making compost (and talking about wiggly worms making tunnels in the garden to help feed the seed babies) or growing a few vegetables (that your child can pick and eat raw or help you prepare for cooking), they will become environmentally conscious.

'We go on lots of walks. I love to talk to the kids about the things we see along the way. They learn so much from that – the first two learned to count in odds and evens from mailbox numbers, and know a wide variety of plants. The middle two and I tend to our chooks each day.'

Bronni

'My two-and-a-half-year-old is obsessed with bugs. Millipedes are his favourite. He would collect them all day if he could. At first he'd bring in dozens every day but I think he's culled the local population because he is lucky to come inside with three a day now. So, we go to the park to get millipedes, or when we go to his sister's kinder, we raid their supply. I am glad his fascination with snails is over though, because I was sick of finding crushed snails on my sofas and dried up snails (no shells) all over the place. He also loves trucks, trains, cars and blocks, but somehow the millipedes end up playing train rides. They are a big part of our life right now!'

Jacqui

Enjoying nature with your toddler

✿ Help your child become aware of the changes in nature by creating a nature table with a colourful cloth to match the seasons (green in spring, rose pink in summer, orange in autumn and dark blue in winter), and pictures and seasonal objects on top (blossoms, paper butterflies and chickens in spring; yellowing leaves, berries and seed pods, and perhaps a small hollowed pumpkin with a candle inside in autumn; shells and driftwood in summer; bare branches and cut-out snowflakes in winter). Encourage your child to add objects he collects while out and about, such as beautiful stones, shells, sticks, leaves, seed pods, feathers and pieces of lamb's wool.

❀ Let your child have his own garden and help him put in quick-growing plants such as nasturtiums, cosmos, marigolds, cornflowers, sunflowers or geraniums, or seedlings of vegetables like beans, radishes, cherry tomatoes, lettuce, pumpkin, zucchini or potatoes. Children can become discouraged by early failure, so opt for plants that are easy to grow.

❀ Designate a small patch of the yard where children are free to dig in the dirt, add water, make 'rivers' and bridges with planks, small logs and stones, squish and mix, stomp, squelch and generally be messy. Rinse them off before they come back inside!

❀ Make objects from nature: necklaces from flowers (daisy chains) or seed pods threaded together; a bird feeder from a pine cone rolled in honey and seeds then hung from a branch in the garden; boats from walnut shells with paper or leaf sails stuck in place with clay or Blu-Tack (put a few rocks in a bowl, add some water and sail the walnut boats); make mobiles from sticks and seed pods, gum nuts or shells tied to a branch or piece of driftwood.

❀ Take a nature walk and explore your backyard. Lift up

rocks and stones and hunt for creepy crawlies. (Use a magnifying glass to watch them up close.) Follow a line of ants.

❧ Watch a snail creep across a glass plate, noticing the waves on his tummy. Or just allow your child to watch a snail crawl across a footpath.

❧ Take a kite to the park or beach on a windy day.

❧ Visit a lake or pond and feed the ducks or watch other water birds such as pelicans.

❧ Make a net with a wire coat hanger and old pantyhose to catch 'fish' (pretend fish are just fine) in a pond or bathtub.

❧ Throw sticks (boats) into a stream and watch them float.

❧ Go to the beach and hunt for 'treasure'. Look in rock-pools, make a sandcastle, watch the tide come in and make footprints then watch them fill with water.

Reading to your toddler

Little children love your focused attention as they snuggle on your lap and listen to a story. As you share these special moments of closeness, your toddler will feel safe and loved as he enters the magic world of stories, and he will be developing his vocabulary and his ability to make patterns of speech and thought. He will make associations between pictures and words and the creatures and objects you are reading about. Gradually, he will learn how stories work and he will begin to create his own stories and 'read' to himself.

Children's author Mem Fox, who is also the author of *Reading Magic* (a fabulous book for parents about instilling a love of reading in their child), offers ten commandments about reading aloud to your toddler:

1. Spend at least ten wildly happy minutes *every single day* reading aloud.
2. Read at least three stories a day: it may be the same story three times. Children need to hear a thousand stories before they learn to read!
3. Read aloud with animation. Listen to your own voice and don't be dull, flat or boring. Hang loose and be loud, have fun and laugh a lot.
4. Read with joy and enjoyment: real enjoyment for yourself and great joy for the listeners.
5. Read the stories that kids love – over and over and over again, and always read in the same 'tune' for each book: that is, with the same intonations on each page, each time.

6. Let children hear lots of language by talking to them constantly; or sing any old song that you can remember; or say nursery rhymes in a bouncy way; or be noisy together doing clapping games.

7. Look for rhyme, rhythm or repetition in books for young children, and make sure the books are short!

8. Play games with the things that you and your child can see on the page, such as finding the letters that start your child's name and yours, remembering that it's never work, it's always a fabulous game.

9. Never ever *teach* reading, or get tense around books.

10. Read aloud every day because you just love being with your child, not because it's the right thing to do.

Television and video games

There is no avoiding it: we live in an electronically driven world. And while few of us could imagine living without technology, we do need to be conscious of how small children are affected by computers, televisions and video games. In many homes, the television is blaring away day and night, and parents seem unaware how this can inhibit children's play, negatively affect their behaviour and communication skills (speech is learned through interaction), dull their senses and affect their ability to sleep well.

Consider, would you allow a badly mannered or violent stranger into your house as a role-model for your child? Unsupervised and unmonitored television viewing or exposure to video games is allowing exactly that to happen. Scary images and loud, angry voices on the television can be upsetting to small children. And advertising targeted at small children can show tots whining for everything from junk food to expensive and unnecessary toys.

A statement published by the American Academy of Paediatrics recommends no television viewing at all for children under two years. While this may seem idealistic or perhaps unrealistic for many families, it is worth considering how you are using television: there are some great children's programs, and half an hour of 'Play School' may allow you to feed the baby or prepare a meal in peace, but a little goes a long way. Television is better watched for short periods with supervision or as an occasional treat, rather than parking your child in front of a screen to keep him out of your way because you feel pressured. I am quite dismayed at how many parents use a DVD player as entertainment in the car. While it may be a boon for older children on a long car journey, small children benefit far more from looking out the window, singing or talking with parents and taking breaks to stretch.

Try to get into the habit of turning the television off when you aren't watching it. This way, you won't be allowing your child to be either lulled into a stupor or hyped-up by the flashing lights (they don't call it the idiot box without good reason); you will be encouraged to interact and attend consciously to your toddler and she will be more motivated to play and learn. This, in turn, will encourage brain development, learning and positive behaviour.

'Television is a treat, and not something we watch without good reason. We can't find enough decent programs to warrant it being on for more than thirty minutes each day anyway. Our children know that it is a special rest period, a block of time to watch something we choose together, which they find fun or educational, or a bit of both. Sometimes it's Play School, other times a documentary about animals. Last week, we watched a special on hot air balloons, which they found fascinating. Limiting our time with the television means that our children aren't bombarded with clever marketing to make them want things, and that they aren't watching fast-flashing images which have been scientifically proven to be harmful to their developing brains.

'Being with them when they are watching a program means

they can ask questions about things they see. We can also keep an eye on what they are watching. We've given up on having the TV on at all during news time, as we don't think that the content is suitable for small people.

'We love to see how delighted they are when we have quiet time together on the beanbags or couch. Our oldest son, who has just turned three, claps his hands and cheers. For daily "noise" we play CDs, open the windows and listen to the sounds of nature, or simply cherish the sounds that small people playing with toys make when left to their own devices.'

Donna

'Before our first child was born, we chose to get rid of our television. Our home became much more peaceful and relaxing. Our quality of life was enriched as we found other ways to spend our time, like talking and enjoying each other's company, spending time with friends, doing craft and reading good books. Our home became a more wholesome place in which to nurture a child. We were able to focus attention on her more fully.

'Many people ask us what we do to entertain ourselves and our children without a television in our house. We have lots of things to occupy our time. Our children enjoy playing together, and we often make a cubby with blankets over chairs for them to play in. If I give them some mixing bowls and utensils they *love clanging around and pretending to make things. We also use playdough, draw, do simple crafts, read, dance, play with musical instruments, go for walks and visit friends.*

'I involve them in household tasks and they love to help. They like mixing or chopping when I'm cooking, dipping the dishes in rinsing water, handing me things from the basket when I'm hanging out the washing, and helping put things away. It sometimes makes jobs take longer, but when we do things together it makes mundane tasks more fun. On warm days, I give each of my children a large bowl of water, some cups and containers, and let them play outside. '

'Children are ingenious and creative little beings and will make a game out of just about anything, so we never feel like we are missing out by not having television. On the contrary, I feel like my children are having a very enriching childhood with lots of hands-on play and fun and games!'

Alice

Toddler tactic: playtime inspiration

Copy this list and paste it on your fridge to refer to in desperate moments or when you have severe 'mummy brain'.

❀ **Make an obstacle course indoors or out.** *Climb over cushions and through cardboard boxes, walk along a plank* supported on phone books or bricks, or balance on a hose curled across the lawn.

✿ **Get physical.** *March, jump, hop or skip, kick or throw a ball, walk to the shops, around the block, in the rain and stomp in puddles or collect leaves, sticks, gum nuts or rocks on the way.*

✿ **Play hide and seek.** *Take turns hiding and finding your tot or hide a toy and let her find it. If your child understands, tell her when she is getting 'warmer' (close) or 'cool' (not near the hidden object).*

✿ **Pretend.** *Set up a shop with empty packets and bottle lids for play money, a hair salon with brushes, capes and an old hair dryer with the electrical cord cut off, or a hospital with Band Aids, 'sick' teddies and dolls, and a toy stethoscope.*

✿ **Build.** *Use blocks, cartons and boxes, old sheets draped over a card table or pegged to a tree to make cubbies.*

✿ **Play in water.** *Shallow water in an old baby bath is fun (with careful supervision) and it can be emptied on the garden for the plants to drink later. Give your child empty containers to fill and pour, a colander, squirty plastic bottles, an eggbeater or whisk.*

✿ **Paint the fence.** *Use water in a bucket and a wide paintbrush. This game will last for ages as you enjoy some quiet time having a cuppa nearby!*

❀ **Plant some seeds.** *You can set up a spot outside, or plant inside using jars or saucers. Carrot tops will grow in a saucer, and cress seeds grow hair for eggshell people. To make them, use half an eggshell with a face drawn on in texta, then fill with wet cotton wool – the cress will grow into long green hair.*

❀ **Sing and dance.** *Put on some music, swing scarves or coloured lengths of ribbon tied onto plastic bangles, bring out the instrument box, and boogie!*

Chapter six
Routines and rituals

The only real certainty in your toddler's life is that there are changes every day: there is so much development going on for your child that even in a stable, consistent environment, her world will be ever-evolving as she learns new skills and makes new discoveries. Toddlers feel safe and secure when they know what they can count on, and where their place is in the big, exciting world. Your little one will blossom when there is order and simplicity. She feels good when there is a predictable rhythm to her days, and she is more likely to cooperate with you because she isn't stressed and confused by chaos. This doesn't mean you have to become a rigid clock watcher ('No, poppet, I can't watch you take your first step. Remember, after breakfast I do the dishes while you play with your blocks!'). The odds are that as your baby becomes a toddler, she will naturally settle into a fairly predictable daily rhythm. Whether this is quite relaxed, or more precisely organised, will depend on your family situation and your individual child, and whatever is most comfortable for all of you.

One caution around routines is that if they are extremely rigid, you may find your child becomes quite upset if there are any variations or times of change. On the other hand, when you have a more flexible rhythm marked by rituals at transitions such as mealtimes, bedtime and going out times, and you give your child little reminders as these transitions are approaching ('It's nearly time to wash our hands for dinner'), you will find it easier to manage your day. You may also find you have a more adaptable child if some days the order of things is a bit different, as long as he isn't stretched unreasonably beyond his regular meal and rest times.

'With four children under nine, routines could not exist for my third child. Between school drop-offs, kinder pick-ups and after-school activities, he was in and out of car seats, prams and slings. Routines for him revolve around sleeps, play, eating, baths, even nappy changes. I understand that routines are about forming positive habits that encourage the child to behave habitually but the time is not spent together. I found that routine was doing something to or for my children, not with them. I had to find another way to give my toddler meaningful positive experiences.

'We came up with games called Little Rituals, and they became part of our sharing time together. They were played religiously, forming a ceremonial act and often enjoyed by the siblings and other family members, too. The ritual games were met with excitement and anticipation. There was mutual joy and communal celebration. Routines provide rewards for the parents (peace of mind, quiet time while toddler sleeps etc), while our rituals were personal and focused on our child's needs. Our rituals were not dictated by the clock. They were dictated by the desire to make a memory that was based on fun and interaction. We could be in the car and I would sing a song that required my boy to echo, or present a bedtime bear and we'd both sing a lullaby. My husband would hug our boy and make him laugh off to sleep. We continue to create our own unique family rituals – our own culture, if you like.'

Jo

Your daily rhythm

Most families with small children have a basic daily rhythm. Yours may be influenced by your child's morning wake-up time, how many sleeps your child needs, whether both parents work outside the home, and whether you have school-age children with set drop-off and pick-up times.

You will also have a weekly rhythm that revolves around shopping days, regular appointments, visiting friends and extended family, and activities such as playgroup or toddler classes.

If one parent is the full-time carer, a typical day could look like this:

Waking, dressing and breakfast. Mornings follow the order that works best for your individual family.

Housework. Chores are done with some 'help' from your toddler, or you set him up with an activity nearby.

Toddler tactic: get the day off to a good start

Set up an activity the night before as a morning surprise. Put out a new book or a different toy on a low bookshelf or in 'his' cupboard (keep one kitchen cupboard especially for your child so he can play near you as you do chores).

You can combine chores with outdoor play or an excursion by taking your toddler outside as you hang out washing or walk to the shops. Rather than being rigid, follow his lead – if your child seems ready to be outdoors or plays better after a romp, work around this, perhaps reversing the suggestions here for housework and outdoor play times.

Morning tea. If breakfast has been very early, a mid-morning snack (which may be as early as 9 a.m.) will refuel your toddler and raise blood sugar levels and he will play more pleasantly. This will allow you to prepare his lunch – it is always efficient to stay one step ahead rather than try and wrestle a tired or hungry child as you fiddle round making food or finding clothes or equipment for the next activity.

Outdoor activity. You might take a walk together, or go to playgroup, swim, gym or music class. Physical activity in the morning often helps children become more settled later – read, worn out and ready for quieter play. Note: classes and excursions will become weekly rhythms that can be anticipated by rituals such as singing familiar songs (perhaps a song that is sung at his class) as your child gets ready.

Lunch. Sit together and eat. You may say a mealtime blessing or sing a song of thanks and light a candle before eating.

Story and rest or quiet time. If your toddler has outgrown an afternoon nap, it is a good idea to have some quiet play as part of your daily rhythm – you will benefit from a period of relaxation, too! Set up a space for quiet time (either in the family room or your child's room if it isn't isolated from you) with a beanbag or large cushions, a soft rug and a basket of quiet toys such as books. Quiet time could consist of block play, looking through photo albums (make your child his own small albums if you are concerned he may damage photos) or picture books, doing simple puzzles, craft activities (small children can calmly focus their energy while stringing large wooden beads or sorting coloured blocks or buttons into a muffin tray – with careful supervision if parts are small) or drawing with crayons (they are a more satisfying sensory activity than felt-tipped pens and aren't as messy – here's a tip: cooking oil and a paper towel will wipe crayon off walls).

Afternoon tea. Maintaining your child's and your own blood sugar levels can make for early-evening harmony instead of a pre-dinner arsenic hour. And if you offer light, healthy snacks and drinks (such as water and fruit, rather than cookies and milk), his appetite at dinner won't be spoiled. Take a break yourself and eat or drink with your toddler. You will keep your own energy levels steady and he will be in a much more civilised mood to greet the parent who is returning home.

Play or walk. An afternoon walk will help release endorphins (in you and your toddler) and allow you some lovely time together before the evening rush.

Dinner. Prepare the evening meal with your child's

'help' if she is old enough; otherwise, set her up with her own cooking utensils at a low table or cupboard. When it's time to eat, sit with your child and have a snack or drink with her. If you eat together as a family, please don't make this too late or your toddler will be 'past it'.

Family time. You may enjoy a quiet game, a walk together or a massage (see Pizza massage instructions, page 136). If your toddler is younger and gets tired early, it may be best to incorporate family time into your dinner, bathing or bedtime preparation.

Bath. This can be a lovely time to share with the partner who works outside the home. As well as being great bonding and play time, a shower or bath together saves time and water!

Bedtime. This most commonly includes changing into pyjamas, brushing teeth, reading a story and giving lots of cuddles.

Parents' time. Bring out the chocolates!

If parents work outside the home and children are in childcare, a typical day could look like this:

Waking, dressing and breakfast.

Parent takes the child to childcare then heads off to work.

Pick up child. Create your own special 'hello' ritual.

Connecting time. Spend some special time together, enjoying a romp in the park, a play or a shared snack or bath. It can be hard to factor in some bonding time when you've rushed from work to childcare and the evening meal is still uncooked, but it's very important to find even a few minutes to reconnect with your child.

Dinner. If time allows, let your toddler 'help' (breaking beans, cracking eggs, buttering bread with a blunt knife – a three-year-old could even set the table). Otherwise, set your toddler up with an activity near you. If there are two parents at home, one could play with your child or do bath time while the other one cooks.

Eat together as often as you can. Maintaining rituals such as saying a blessing or talking about your day is very connecting and grounding, whether your child has been separated from you during the day or whether he has been cared for by one parent at home.

Family time. Play, walk, read or consider bath time as family time if your little one is really tired and needs to get to bed.

Bedtime. Changing into pyjamas, brushing teeth, reading a story and giving lots of cuddles!

Parents' time. Again, dessert!

Good mornings

While we are usually prepared to acknowledge the benefits of a gentle bedtime rhythm, we don't always consider that the sensory experience of waking is also a major transition. Think of a typical busy household in the morning with blaring alarm clocks, television news with images of disaster and mayhem, and parents and siblings rushing around. By creating a gentle beginning to the day, stress levels can plummet for you and your child. So why not work out a morning rhythm that works for you both?

'Hattie comes into bed with us when she wakes in the morning. She has a big breastfeed and then plays "Where's Hattie?" under the doona. When she is ready for breakfast, Dad takes her down to the kitchen and they eat together, while Mum reads the paper in bed over a cup of tea, and listens! Bliss.'

Kate

'I feel so privileged that I don't have to rush off to work in the mornings and can share that special time with our little ones. Our three-year-old came into our bed this morning and asked, "Who is God?" I'm not sure which part of my explanation

appealed to him as he nodded and said, "Oh, so he's like Bob the Builder."'

Jenny

Here are some ideas to make mornings with your toddler more relaxed:

✿ If you aren't a morning person, try shifting your own bedtime back half an hour or so (gradually), so you can ease yourself awake. If your sanity, like mine, depends on reading late at night when the house is quiet, skip this bit – just keep the alarm volume low so yours are the only assaulted senses.

✿ Create a special way to greet the morning before your child wakes, with a cuppa, some yoga or meditation. If your child is a 5 a.m. waker, pull the blankets over your head and pretend to be asleep as long as you dare. Too long though, and he may be creating mayhem in the kitchen!

✿ If your toddler is an early riser, why not do some yoga or meditation *together*, or go outside and greet the day. There is no excuse to prop them in front of the television (except for weekend sleep-ins: video hire was invented for parental respite under exceptional circumstances!).

On weekend mornings, or when you want some extra zzzs, try leaving a surprise basket beside your toddler's bed – a drink in a lidded cup, a safe snack, a picture book and a toy.

❀ Avoid a morning rush by preparing the night before: make snacks or lunches, fill water bottles, lay out clothes, and if you are planning to go out or to work in the morning, leave everything you need in a spot by the door.

❀ Gently welcome your child from the womblike world of sleep with a special greeting. If you have a nice singing voice (or your toddler is more forgiving than mine were!), sing a morning song or play some quiet, happy music.

❀ Create rituals around breakfast, dressing, hair-brushing and teeth-cleaning.

❀ Give your children special morning hugs and make eye contact as you tell them how much you love them.

Rushing your toddler

It may seem convenient when little ones comply with our busy schedules, but if you are expecting your toddler to keep up with a highly powered adult timetable, she could sense this hurrying as rejection. Little ones can find it hard to feel valued and cared for when the people they love most don't have time to listen and validate their feelings or meet their needs at their pace. Also, by forcing toddlers to fit in with the demands of our lives, we often rush them into dealing with separations and disturbing situations that they aren't really ready for.

It might be time to consider some more balance in your busy life if you:

❀ feel you are always rushing and your child must 'fit in' with your lifestyle
❀ find yourself justifying and rationalising child-care arrangements even though your child is clearly unhappy
❀ find yourself thinking ahead rather than enjoying the moments with your toddler.

When we add extra stress to toddlers' lives, they need to compensate in some way to cope. They may switch off and become disinterested in playing or mixing with other children or become clingy, whiny or demanding to get your attention. If you can respect your child's rhythm as you plan your day, you will ease the stress in his world, he will feel more outgoing and confident, and his little mind will be available for important tasks such as playing and learning.

Family rituals

As I have mentioned, your day doesn't have to run like clockwork, but a fairly predictable rhythm marked with rituals will bring comfort and connection as you share family time with love and reverence amid the chaos of everyday life.

We all have different priorities and values to share with our children, and these can be reflected in daily rituals such as saying a blessing or lighting a candle before sharing meals or singing a special bedtime song; weekly rituals such as fish and chip night, pancake breakfasts on Saturday, or Sunday lunch with extended family; seasonal rituals such as spring cleaning or raking autumn leaves; and, of course, special celebrations such as birthdays and holidays.

'We eat all our meals together, at the table. It is such a lovely way to bond. We generally make the meal together, eat together and pack up together. We have a no-TV rule during the week, so on weekends we'll watch a movie together while

eating pizza. Another ritual we have is goodnight and good morning kisses all round.'

Mandy

As well as creating your own unique family culture and cementing family bonds, there are documented benefits from implementing family rituals: after reviewing fifty years of research, psychologists at New York's Syracuse University concluded that families who reported following routines such as eating together, bedtime lullabies, birthday celebrations and meals with extended family enjoyed some important health benefits such as better overall children's health, increased marital satisfaction and less stress.

Creating rituals

❀ **Examine your day.** Which activities are habitual and which do you and your child enjoy (or find a challenge)? Consider how you can invest your time together with meaning, with a favourite song, a candle, or perhaps a specific activity before or after work.

❀ **Take it slowly.** Too many changes can be as chaotic as no rituals at all. Waking and bedtime are significant transitions, so these are a good starting point for creating rituals.

❀ **Look to your own childhood.** What were your happiest celebrations? How can you weave this magic for your own child?

❀ **Celebrate your uniqueness.** Your rituals are a part of what identifies you as a family, so throw out preconceived ideas if they don't suit and celebrate your individuality. If both parents are from different cultural backgrounds, for instance, mix your own blend of celebrations as you expose your children to the richness of both extended families.

Everyday magic

Stop and consider, what are you doing *with* your children? Are your days all drudgery and instructions, activities and material goodies to keep little ones entertained as you race against the clock, or do you make time to share magic moments? I'm not advocating that as well as all the 'to dos' you also have to be a wand-waving wonder mummy, weaving magic spells into every waking moment of your child's day. What I'm advocating is simple – benevolent neglect (well, almost). Throw off the performance anxiety involved in 'doing it all' (whatever 'all' means to you) and try giving yourself and your child a moment to breathe and enjoy the wonder that is a natural part of every day.

Keeping things simple and helping children see the magic in life takes minimal effort (and expense) besides slowing down, seeing things through a child's eyes and celebrating the wonder of each day. Enchantment relieves boredom for you and your child, and appreciating simple moments will create memories and nourish your child's creative spirit. This is a lasting gift that will sustain your child as he or she grows beyond her carefree childhood. Your toddler will remember seeing a train or truck up close for the very first time (please resist the urge to explain how steam is made or point out the great big wheels – allow your child to be captivated by her own sense of awe); taking bread to feed the ducks; listening to the sea in a shell held to her ear; tasting the rain; jumping in puddles; or looking for fairies in the soap bubbles as you do dishes.

As you encourage your child's magical spirit, it is equally important to model whatever nurtures your own spirit – light an oil burner; put on music and dance (with your child, your partner or a glorious silk scarf – or all of the above!); make a pot of tea and drink out of a delicate china cup (it may be a tea party with your child or you could have a quiet drink outside as you watch him play);

sing out loud (silly songs in the car or an uplifting song to make your own spirit soar); take off your shoes and feel the sand, grass or earth underfoot; lie under a tree with your toddler and relax as you watch the leaves; say yes when your child requests your help to make a cubby or dress up in a funny costume – you may find yourself infused with childish abandon and enchantment (the 'to-dos' will wait, I promise!).

Toddler tactic: make magic

❀ *Make up magical stories about seasons. Become aware of the uniqueness of nature each season and share this with your child: in spring, sprout a seed and talk about elves cleaning each petal to make the garden sparkle; in summer, tell the story of Puck from* A Midsummer Night's Dream, *watch the waves melt a sandcastle, go berrypicking then make jam together; in autumn, jump in the leaves; in winter, go for a walk by candlelight, and bake some potatoes or damper in a bonfire.*

❀ *Encourage children to make fairy houses in the garden. Let them make little gifts for elves and fairies – tiny cakes, little hats from playdough or beeswax (buy coloured moulding wax from craft shops), a miniature picture or a tiny blanket from fabric scraps.*

✿ *Leave gifts from the elves and fairies in return – a gum nut, some chocolate chips, a fairy sticker or a daisy chain deco-ration left in your child's bedroom. Perhaps a gift could be placed inside a daisy chain. Of course, you'll know if the fairies have visited because there'll be a trail of fairy dust (glitter).*

✿ *Don't always read stories to your children. Make some up. Little ones love to hear stories about nature, the weather, themselves, and the 'olden days' when you were a child.*

✿ *Find the magical in ordinary things like gardening, driving, cooking and so on. Tell stories or share a moment of won-der. Notice the rainbows and sunsets.*

Chapter seven
Let's eat

Mealtimes are about so much more than just food. As nurturers of our children we are responsible for their eating habits and health. Our own relationship with food can also colour our perspective and make mealtimes fraught with anxiety or a relaxed, pleasant time of family connection.

It can be quite confronting to admit how much influence we have on our children's eating habits because it may require some drastic changes on our part. For instance, what makes up the bulk of your own diet? Do you eat mainly processed foods? Do you consume junk food or soft drinks as a normal part of your daily diet? How do the foods you eat, and the packaging they come in, impact on the environment? Do you sit and enjoy meals and share conversation with your partner and children or do you eat on the run? Do you eat at the table or sitting in front of television? It is up to us as parents to create the culture of mealtimes within our home. Although genteel dining complete with perfect manners (and a clean floor beneath the table) is a while off yet, you can sow the seeds for a healthy attitude towards eating and create mealtimes where food is served and enjoyed with love and reverence, not nagging, bribing and stress. It isn't worth creating stress over your toddler's table manners if you want her to experience mealtimes as a pleasant time of family connection. She will naturally copy your own polite example as she develops motor and language skills and impulse control.

'We're not religious, but we do have a few rituals which we try to abide by. The most important one is for us to wait until everyone is seated before we pick up our cutlery to start eating. When our eldest son was quite small, we'd make a point of thanking whoever it was who had made the meal. For example, my husband would say, "Thanks, Mummy, for cooking our lovely dinner," and our son would copy. Now, especially when it is a meal he really loves, he is the first to pipe up and say something similar. It's so nice to take him out and hear him thank others for his food without being asked, and to see how much pleasure that brings to the person receiving the gratitude. Simple manners can mean so much. We also excuse ourselves from the table. If we are busy and don't have time to sit and wait for everyone to finish, we do that as it feels polite and respectful. We have the television in another room, but *sometimes we'll play a CD. It doesn't take a lot to make family mealtimes special, so we make an effort for it to be a time when we share what we've all done, and enjoy each other's company.'*

Donna

Family foods

A lot of confusion arises around feeding as your chubby baby becomes a toddler: although he is now very active, the rapid growth of your toddler's first year will slow down and his appetite may decrease accordingly. He will also be so busy exploring his world or playing with his toys and practising his new physical skills that he may simply have better things to do than stop and eat. As well as less interest in food, your toddler's limited concentration span will mean it is unrealistic to expect him to sit at a table for a three-course meal (unless it can be eaten in minutes!). His eating behaviour will seem erratic as his appetite tends to fluctuate from day to day – he may have an 'eating day' followed by several days when he seems less hungry. Also, in the second year it is common for little ones to use food (or refusal of food) to assert their developing independence.

Because of your toddler's small appetite, it is important

to make sure that the foods you do offer are not 'empty' fillers that will affect his appetite for more healthy food (and no, tomato sauce doesn't count as a vegetable!). Try to include a wide variety of foods in as close to their nat-ural state as possible. This means eating fresh fruit and vegetables, wholegrains, fish, meats and free-range eggs, and drinking water or milk, instead of filling your toddler with processed foods such as chicken nuggets, coloured 'yoghurts', biscuits, flavoured milk or cordial.

But don't stress about every morsel that your child eats because he hasn't had a required daily intake or sampled every food group in a single day. Remember, you can't worry your toddler into eating – your anxiety is more likely to have the opposite effect. However, if you do feel concerned about your child's eating patterns, try keeping a food diary for a week. You may be pleasantly surprised to find that over a week he is eating a reasonably healthy amount and variety of food.

To encourage healthy eating:
- **Turn off the television** while you eat.
- **Adapt food** from family meals or at least prepare foods for your child that you will enjoy if he doesn't eat up. If you haven't slaved over a hot stove for hours preparing tiny

gourmet meals, you won't feel personally rejected if your tot turns his nose up at them. Or try a slight variation: if your child doesn't like rice try couscous; if they won't eat pumpkin or carrot try blending it into a risotto.

❀ **Nutritious snacks** are important for busy little bodies who don't manage three big meals a day. Healthy snacks will help prevent mood swings and difficult behaviour due to low blood sugar levels. Take snacks and a water bottle when you go out so you don't resort (too often, at least) to junk food to appease hungry tots.

❀ **Offer finger foods**: your child can feed herself independently by choosing what and how much she eats if you allow her healthy choices such as pieces of soft fruit, bread or small sandwiches, lightly steamed or grated vegetables, or cheese segments. (See also Safe eating, page 184.)

❀ **Introduce new foods one at a time**, serving a new food along with some familiar ones, gradually increasing the amount of the new food. You can keep an eye out for allergies or other adverse reactions (diarrhoea, sore tummy) by changing your toddler's diet slowly.

❀ **Encourage your toddler to feed himself** and praise him when he manages to get food onto his spoon and tries to eat it. You may need to have two spoons (one for you and one for your child) for a just-turned one-year-old so that you can put some food into his mouth between his own sloppy attempts. If he loses interest in the spoon (read, throws it overboard) continue feeding him yourself until he signals he has eaten enough. As your child 'gets it' and tries to feed himself, gradually decrease the amount of help you give him – it will be messy at first but he needs practice to become an independent eater.

❁ **Praise your child when she sits still** in her highchair. It is common for one-year-olds to go through a stage of hating to sit still, so you will need to have food absolutely ready before you attempt to seat her and try distracting her by drawing her attention to the food, her spoon or candles on the table before she starts her 'performance'. To help her feel more 'included' (rather than trapped in her chair), remove the tray of the highchair and push her up close to the table if possible.

❁ **Don't put too much food on your child's plate.** Try to make food look attractive and fun by doing simple things like serving half a kiwifruit in an egg cup, cutting sandwiches into shapes using cookie cutters, or asking children to choose something of each colour (as they name it) from a platter. You might like to arrange the food on your platter into a face or animal shape, using egg, sultanas, carrot sticks, cheese cubes and so on.

❀ **Make meals extra special** (at least sometimes) by lighting candles or having a picnic – in the backyard, in the park, with friends, on long trips or inside on cold or rainy days.

❀ **Let your toddler help prepare food.** She could break vegetables, add herbs, stir and taste – if you are preparing healthy foods it really doesn't matter if some is eaten before she gets to the table.

❀ **Try not to encourage negative behaviour** by laughing or fussing if your toddler spits or throws food or tries to stand on her chair. Remove the food until she settles down and if she refuses food and begins to play, assume that mealtime is over, wipe her hands and take her out of her chair.

'Our three-year-old daughter has never been overly interested in dinner. But dinner is when we usually eat important vegetables. If we make dinner, serve it up and expect her to eat, it rarely works. But when we let her help to cook, whether she washes some vegetables or puts cut-up pieces in the pot, she is much more enthusiastic about eating. She will also eat bits of uncooked vegetables while we are preparing the meal. So

even if she doesn't eat much of the finished product, we know she has had a good dose of nutritious vegetables.

'We have also found that eating meals with loved family members, such as Grandma, means that she will eat all of her meal.'

Linda

'I have found a few great tricks to make sure food goes down the hatch. The first trick is to drizzle veggies with homemade gravy (no rubbish-laden powders that you mix with water) when kids are feeling a bit fussy. Also, when I have vegetables to use up that don't look appealing or that I know are not favourites, I grate them in a food processor and mix them with savoury mince or spaghetti bolognaise. After a bit of cooking, and perhaps a bit of low-salt soy sauce to cover the colours up and a bit of spice (coriander works well), we have a huge meal that gives us leftovers that can be frozen, and there is not a scrap left on anyone's plate.'

Sonia

Healthy snacks

Tiny tummies don't need to be filled with sweet biscuits and chips – these can cause tooth decay as well as disrupt little appetites. Although active children will 'burn off' sweets and an occasional treat won't hurt, the longer your toddler takes to learn about sweets, the easier it will be for you – she won't miss (or demand) what she doesn't know about. Of course, a second or subsequent child may not remain innocent for long, so make the most of it. Remember, you have the 'keys' to the food cupboard, even if you may have to gently explain this to grandparents.

Some healthy snacks for toddlers:

- ✿ **Fresh fruits** such as banana, watermelon, rockmelon or soft pears.
- ✿ **Tiny sandwiches** cut into shapes to look attractive.
- ✿ **Toast strips** made from different breads. Fruit breads can be a nice treat.
- ✿ **Yoghurt,** which can also be a dip for fruit slices.
- ✿ **Wholegrain breakfast cereal.** Be sure to choose one low in sugar and salt.
- ✿ **Pita bread, crackers or breadsticks** served with lightly steamed veggies, dip or cream cheese.
- ✿ **Homemade muffins** with added berries, grated carrot or fruit.
- ✿ **Little pancakes** made using different flours such as buckwheat or a mix of white and wholemeal.

Cold cooked pasta makes a good finger food for tiny hands.

Toddler tactic: provide healthy snacks

If you want to buy snacks for your toddler, take care to read the ingredients labelling – ingredients are listed in order of how much of each is in the food. So if the first ingredient listed is sugar (which may also be called dextrose or sucrose), this is the main ingredient in the food. Many so-called 'health foods' are full of sugar and have a high fat or salt content. They also often have additives such as artificial colouring or flavours. Most processed snack foods have very small amounts of anything healthy (such as wholegrains or fruit) and can negatively affect your child's appetite for unprocessed foods that are really healthy. Sweet foods can damage tiny teeth and affect your child's behaviour, making him hyper as he gets a sugar hit then cranky as he is let down soon after. It is best to avoid these, but if you do get caught short with a hungry child, why not buy a truly healthy snack food such as a banana?

Safe eating

Toddlers need to be supervised whenever they are eating to avoid accidents and choking.

✿ Avoid falls from highchairs by using straps to contain your child safely, and check that straps are properly fastened every time you use them so your tot can't slide out.

✿ Make sure the highchair is placed out of reach of foods that can be pulled over as well as hazards such as kettles, hot water, hot plates and curtain or blind cords.

✿ Teach little ones to sit – not stand – on chairs by repeatedly sitting them and saying a simple word such as 'safe' or 'bottoms on seats'. If they keep standing, take them off the chair and place them on the floor. Try to be relaxed but firm and don't make a fuss by growling or shouting as this will encourage them to climb even more. Remember, little ones don't give a hoot whether your reaction is positive or negative as long as they have your attention. Some children are natural climbers so you may have to move chairs out of reach (make sure they are slid under the table after meals) if you can't supervise constantly.

✿ Back teeth needed to chew and grind harder foods may not be fully developed until around four years; food swallowed in large pieces is more likely to get stuck and block off airways, and running around, laughing or crying while toddlers are eating is likely to increase the risk of choking. To reduce the risk of choking, make sure small children are sitting quietly as they eat and never force a child to eat.

✿ Don't give your toddler foods that can break off into hard pieces such as raw carrot, celery sticks, apple pieces and hard pears. Instead, lightly steam or cook hard vegetables and fruits or offer grated carrot and apple.

✿ Avoid giving popcorn, nuts, hard lollies and corn chips to toddlers. Nuts are potentially dangerous to children under four.

✿ Cut grapes in half, so they don't slide down whole and block tiny airways. At about four years, they can usually eat grapes whole.

✿ Avoid giving sausages and frankfurts. When you introduce these to older tots, peel skins off and cut them into small pieces so children won't gag on lumps that are perfectly sized to catch in little airways.

✿ Teach older children to check with you before they offer food to your toddler.

For what to do if your child chokes, see the Raising Children Network's website: http://raisingchildren.net.au/articles/pip_choking.html.

Fussy eaters

If you are poised, spoon in hand, performing daring feats to get your toddler to open wide and eat 'just one more spoonful' – *stop*! You are getting yourself into an unnecessary battle that you can't win, and you could be creating longer-term problems. No matter how anxious you feel about your toddler's disinterest in eating, please remind yourself (over and over if necessary) that your toddler won't starve himself if he has access to a variety of healthy foods. The best way to avoid food fights is to remain calm and not be drawn into battle. Without a reaction, you won't risk reinforcing your child's behaviour and he will more quickly get over his fussing.

To keep mealtimes calm:

❀ Don't enter into any discussion about your child's food such as, 'One more for Daddy, the pussycat, the starving millions.'
❀ Keep helpings small and don't fuss if she doesn't eat every mouthful.
❀ Don't use food as a reward or punishment: 'Be good and you can have a lolly,' or 'You can't get out of the highchair until you eat all your dinner.'

❀ Don't substitute food for nurturing, such as giving a biscuit to distract a crying child.

❀ It's common for toddlers to assert their developing independence by saying no to everything at about eighteen months. Try not to react strongly or he will keep doing it.

❀ If your child doesn't like vegetables, don't fight; let him eat fruit (it has the same nutrients, though more sugar) or hide vegetables in pasta sauce, meatballs, pancakes, omelettes or on pizzas (use pita bread as a pizza base).

Toddler tactic: fussy eaters

Cold, lightly cooked vegetables often go down well, especially if you offer a healthy dip such as hommus or avocado. Tomato sauce contains a lot of sugar and salt but, used sparingly, it may make veggies more palatable to a fussy tot. By the way, baked beans are a vegetable that most little ones can't resist!

❀ Don't threaten or bribe your child to eat up, and please don't follow him around as you cajole him to eat. It is your responsibility to provide healthy foods and his to eat (or not). Hungry children eat. If you exert control over food at this age, you convey messages that she can wield food as a weapon. While this may simply mean your wilful toddler clamps his mouth shut now, it can also have longer-term repercussions. Many teenagers who binge, starve or vomit are trying to exert control over their lives by doing something nobody else can influence.

'As long as I offer my children reasonably healthy food, I know I've done my part. If they are hungry they eat, if not they don't. If they decide they only want to eat some of the things on their plate and not others, that's okay, too. But I don't stop offering them something because I think they won't like it. Just because they don't eat something the first few times, doesn't mean they won't like it later on. I serve up the same meal to the whole family regardless, and sometimes they surprise me by eating something they had previously said they didn't like. Food is not an issue in our house because we don't make it one.'

Zoe

The weight game

Toddlers have a wide range of normal growth patterns so if you have a leaner or larger child than average and you feel concerned, it may be reassuring to consider family growth patterns. If you or your partner are small in stature or fine-boned or, conversely, one of you comes from a tall, large-boned family, your child's growth may reflect this family tendency (ask your mum and mother-in-law for your own baby health books).

Breastfed children are often leaner by the time they reach toddlerhood so to allay anxiety about your breastfed toddler's growth, refer to the World Health Organization weight charts (see Resources, page 303). These charts have been developed using breastfeeding infants from several countries as the criteria for normal, rather than a mixture of breast- and formula-fed, mainly Caucasian infants, as many weight charts do.

'I came home from my baby's twelve-month weigh-in at the health centre feeling demoralised and worried. The nurse told me that my toddler was dropping off the weight charts – according to the chart in the baby book she had slipped below the third percentile. I was advised to reduce her breastfeeds so she would eat more food, but that didn't seem to affect her food intake. She eats a really good breakfast after her best breast-feed early in the morning. She is a very active child and has about three breastfeeds most days and I didn't want to reduce these as I feel they are even more important because she is petite. I called a lactation consultant who advised me to compare Charlotte's weight with the WHO charts which are based

on breastfed babies and I was relieved to find she has been
around the twenty-fifth percentile since she was a month old.'

Tania

Of course, if you are genuinely concerned that your child isn't growing well or if he is pale and lethargic as well as disinterested in food, please do have him checked by a health professional.

Allergies and food sensitivity

Itching, coughing, wheezing and sneezing can be a normal part of childhood bugs. However, if any or all of these symptoms continue, they could be a signal that your child has allergies: allergic reactions occur when the immune system reacts abnormally to substances such as dust mites or airborne allergens or foods, and produces antibodies against them. The most common food culprits are cows' milk protein (also found in milk, cheese, butter, icecream and yoghurt), eggs, nuts, fish, wheat, citrus and soy products.

Reactions can vary widely among individuals and allergy symptoms can include rashes, nausea, vomiting or diarrhoea, respiratory congestion and wheezing. In extreme cases, children can have an anaphylactic reaction, which can be life-threatening. If you discover that your child is severely allergic to something, she must avoid all contact with the offending food or substance. This is why many childcare centres will not allow empty food cartons to be brought in for play – in case children who are allergic come into contact with traces of egg or nuts (for example) that may be on packaging.

If you have a child with allergies you will need to educate friends and family to carefully read all food labels and avoid contamination when preparing and serving foods. Just because a food isn't made from a food that your child reacts to, doesn't mean it is safe: foods such as ice-cream, biscuits or breakfast cereals, for instance, may have been processed using equipment that has also been used to make products that contain nuts.

If you or your partner suffer from allergies or there is a family history of eczema, asthma or hay fever, there is an increased likelihood that your child will suffer from allergies. In this case, it is wise to delay the introduction of high-risk foods such as cow's milk, eggs, fish and nut products until after your child is one year old. Also, if you introduce new foods gradually, one at a time, any reactions or sensitivity will be obvious. Of course, if you do suspect your toddler is sensitive or allergic to foods, it would be best to get him checked by a health professional and ask for a referral to a paediatric allergy specialist.

Additives are present in ever-increasing numbers in almost all processed foods and these can also have disruptive effects on little ones' behaviour, causing some children to turn into little monsters. As well as being affected by added chemicals, some tots can become irritable or restless after eating foods containing salicylates. These are naturally occurring chemicals that can be found in otherwise healthy foods such as broccoli, grapes, apples, oranges and tomatoes (as well as in some processed foods).

Food intolerance expert Sue Dengate, who has researched the effects of foods on children's behaviour, including a study into the effects of a common bread preservative, has reported remarkable improvements in children's behaviour with simple dietary changes. These include reducing the amounts of some fruits or changing to bread without preservatives. (See Resources, page 298, for details of Sue's website.)

Because food reactions can vary from an allergic response, which happens very soon after eating a particular food, to an intolerance, which may not show for up to forty-eight hours, it can take some detective work on your part to track down foods that are upsetting your child. In the long run it is worth it, for your sake as well as your child's. If you suspect there is a problem but can't identify the culprit, try keeping a food diary. This doesn't have to be an elaborate exercise: simply write down what your child eats and the time, and note changes in your child's behaviour or physical changes such as rashes or wheezing. You may find, for instance, that the takeaway pizza you have on Friday nights sets off his asthma, or the spaghetti he eats at daycare (which is laden with tomato sauce) makes him 'hyped up'. This way, you will have something tangible to take to your doctor to discuss a treatment plan. Of course, if there is a severe reaction to any food, you will need to seek urgent medical attention.

Mind the milk

Although milk is a nutritious food, toddlers who drink litres of cow's milk at the expense of other foods may be at risk of iron deficiency. Also, milk is very filling so it may diminish your tot's appetite for a wider variety of foods. The recommended milk quota for a toddler is around 600–700 ml a day and this can include yoghurt and cheese. Don't be conned into feeding your child toddler formula.

Despite advertising hype, this is not a substitute for fresh, nutritious food and, because it is very filling (could you eat a decent meal after a thickshake?), it will further disrupt your toddler's appetite.

If your toddler is breastfeeding, you can be more relaxed: you won't know how much milk your little one is drinking and you will probably be making a concerted effort not to sit around nursing all day at this stage. Besides, breast-milk is a nutritious, living food that your child will wean from naturally when he is ready as long as you also offer opportunities to eat family foods. (See Breastfeeding your toddler, page 196.)

One caution is that sucking on a bottle requires a different sucking action from the breast, and continuing to offer bottles to toddlers over the age of two can have negative effects on teeth and jaw development, often requiring serious dental work later. It is also harmful to tiny teeth to have milk from a bottle pooled in the mouth as your little one sleeps (at any age), so if she does have a bedtime bottle, please clean her teeth and remove the bottle before sleep. Although you will need to clean your toddler's teeth if he is breastfed, breastfeeding does not have the same negative effects on dental health as bottle feeding. The sucking action required for breastfeeding actually enhances jaw development so teeth are more likely to be well spaced and, if your child dozes on the breast, milk isn't pooled in her mouth (it hits the back of her throat which means she will swallow rather than having 'leaked' milk sitting around her teeth).

Breastfeeding your toddler

Cultural expectations around how long babies should breastfeed vary quite dramatically: you may be cringing at the thought of a walking, talking child breastfeeding or thinking that only women in primitive countries would nurse a toddler, but the World Health Organization recommends breastfeeding for up to two years and beyond. And worldwide, the average age of weaning toddlers from the breast is four years. Anthropologist Katherine Dettwyler conducted research into the weaning ages of primates and other mammals to determine a 'natural' weaning age for humans. She examined criteria such as length of gestation, age of eruption of permanent teeth and relationship of offspring to adult body size, and made comparisons to average age of weaning in each species. From this she determined that a 'natural' weaning age for humans might be between three and seven years. You can read more about her study in her book *Breastfeeding: Biocultural Perspectives* (see also her website www.kathydettwyler.org).

While breastfeeding a toddler is not everybody's cup of tea (or drink of milk!), knowing that it may be right for your child's natural biology can be reassuring if you are facing criticism. As long as you continue to breastfeed, your child will benefit nutritionally. He will also be protected by the immune factors in your milk as he is exposed to a greater array of bugs through an expanding social life.

Because brain development is incomplete for several years, there is particular interest in the role of breast-milk and children's intelligence levels. One New Zealand study found that children who were breastfed as babies performed better in school and scored higher on standard-ised maths and reading tests – and that the longer they had breastfed, the higher they scored. And, although research into the effects on psychological development is scarce, another New Zealand study which dealt specifically with infants nursed for more than a year, showed fewer behav-ioural problems in six- to eight-year-olds. According to the test results, the longer children had been breastfed, the better they tended to behave.

Mothers, too, benefit from extended breastfeeding. Women who breastfeed for a lifetime total of two years have a reduced risk of developing breast cancer. The risk among mothers who breastfeed for a total of six years or more is reduced by two-thirds, and because maternal bone density increases with each child who is nursed, breast-feeding mothers experience less osteoporosis in later life.

For many mothers of toddlers, breastfeeding isn't just about immunity, intelligence or nutrition, it is also about comfort, pleasure and communication. Breastfeeding is a simple and effective mothering tool, soothing the inevitable knocks and bumps, easing the discomfort of swollen, teeth-ing gums and a pick-me-up when your little one falls – or falls apart emotionally. Often just a few minutes at the breast will reassure toddlers at a deep soulful level. When he was three, one of my own children told me, 'Mummy, booby makes me feel brave, when I get scared.'

'One of the greatest stresses of twin toddlers is when they both need my attention at once, or when they fight with each other. Relief from this was one of the delights of breastfeeding. Then, both boys would snuggle up on my lap for a feed, one sitting on each of my legs and facing each other, and after a little instruc-tion ("Keep your hand on your breast") each boy didn't pester his brother. They would even support each other, like the time when Liam worried, "No milk there!" Francis encouraged him

*to latch on, saying, "Yes there is, there's lots!" and settled down
to feeding on his side. I guess they would have been two years
old then. They eventually weaned about a month apart when
I was pregnant with their little sister.'*

Megan

A breastfed toddler is likely to step up feeds if he is unwell
or out of sorts, perhaps because he is teething or there are
major changes in his life, such as moving house, starting
childcare or going through a developmental leap, but this
will settle naturally when he is over his illness or stress.
If you think your toddler is nursing too much (that is, if
you feel uncomfortable with being constantly 'on tap'), it
is worth looking at what is happening in his (and your) life
and trying to address these possible issues as well as being
a step ahead with nutritious snacks and drinks.

Try to be aware and focused so that your child isn't
breastfeeding simply because he is bored or trying to meet
needs that could be addressed in other ways. He may be
demanding to breastfeed as a means of connecting with
you. Could you involve him in some of your tasks or, better still, slow down and concentrate a little more on him?
Are you away from him more than he is comfortable with?
Are you spending lots of time on the phone or computer

and find him hopping into your lap and 'helping himself'? Are you feeling stressed or upset about events in your own life? Children are sensitive little barometers of our feelings, so you do need to nurture yourself and find support if things are stressful or out of control. If you are consciously parenting but your child still wants to nurse quite often or gets distressed when you try to set limits, you can trust that this is a genuine need and he will outgrow this special closeness when he is ready.

'Around two or two and a half there were times when my daughter seemed to be at the breast so much. Perhaps it was a developmental stage when she needed more reassurance. She is a shy girl and at group gatherings around this time she would often be the only child that was not off playing with the toys. She didn't leave my side and would just breastfeed. Then almost overnight, this clingy constant breastfeeding stopped and, as she headed towards her third birthday, the world and social interaction become much more important to her.

'Her breastfeeding pattern really matched her development. At about two and a half she changed from breastfeeding before sleep to just needing a book and a kiss (this change was purely her doing, not ours, and it happened suddenly).

Toilet training occurred about this time without a fuss. Her playtime with friends underwent a big change from parallel play to imaginative/cooperative play. It makes sense that she no longer wanted to breastfeed a lot when the world of play was beckoning so loudly. Her constant and continual plead from then on has been "play with me" rather than "num-more" (our word for breastfeed).'

Suzanne

Dealing with disapproval

If you sense disapproval from friends and relatives about your feeding choices, remember that you don't owe them an explanation of your child-rearing philosophy – this is your child, your family and your choice. If you simply state the obvious – positively, not apologetically – 'Yes, I am still breastfeeding,' (with a smile) or 'No, I am not breastfeeding,' (with a smile), most people back off. An explanation, on the other hand, may be interpreted as criticism of *their* parenting style. If you are really under pressure to wean and you don't feel like justifying yourself, try bringing out the 'big guns' by saying that your doctor/paediatrician/ lactation consultant (whoever seems most powerful) has advised you to continue breastfeeding.

> ### Toddler tactic: copping it sweet
>
> *If you are facing flack for breastfeeding your toddler, try a cheeky response to deflect your critics:*
>
> **They say:** *'You're not still breastfeeding?'*
> **You say:** *'I'm sorry you can't appreciate the beauty of it.'*
>
> **They say:** *'You'll be going to school to give him lunch.'*
> **You say:** *'Only if I'm on canteen duty.'*
>
> **They say:** *'You'll have to wean him or he'll still want a breast when he's 21.'*
> **You say:** *'Maybe, but it won't be my breast he's after!'*

Weaning your toddler

When to wean your toddler from breast or bottle is a personal choice that will be influenced by your child's readiness and your instincts. Do you know that between one and two years, your toddler will develop what the experts call 'object permanence'. This means that he will be able to carry a picture of you in his mind even when you aren't physically present. This cognitive skill will make weaning easier than weaning a younger child.

You may choose to wean your young toddler from

breast to bottle if you feel he is comforted by sucking or doesn't drink enough fluids from a cup, or you may wean directly from the bottle or breast. If you are weaning a breastfed one-year-old onto a bottle, remember that some of his feeds will have been for comfort rather than 'food' and, although sucking from a bottle will also provide comfort, he won't need as many bottles as he was having breastfeeds.

There are several styles of weaning: you can take the initiative and guide your child to give up breast- or bottle feeding; you can wait for signs that he is less interested and then proactively encourage weaning; or you can trust that when your child is emotionally and physiologically ready, he will wean himself.

'At about nineteen months I weaned Luca from the bottle as I thought some of his (and my) sleep deprivation was due to the habit of waking and using the bottle to get back to sleep. I removed all the bottles and related equipment from sight and that night we gave him milk from a cup and then put him to bed. I knew he could fall asleep without a bottle but he needed a little help that night so I sang to him from the door and through the night I slept on a mattress outside the kids' room. When he woke I would repeat the same phrase, "It's *okay Luca, time for sleep." Sometimes he would fall to sleep again, other times I needed to sing or give him water from a cup. By the third night he was sleeping well. Now he may still wake but usually he can be soothed back to sleep by the same phrase or a sip of water.*

'Weaning from the bottle during the day wasn't a problem. The bottles being out of sight really helped. I offered him milk or water in a cup and he now happily uses a cup all the time.'

Sonia

Ideally, weaning shouldn't be the end of a special bond between you and your child, but rather, a gentle transition to the next stage. This means that however you choose to wean, it will be easier for your toddler (and you) if you make changes gradually, with love. Throwing bottles out in the rubbish or painting your nipples with foul-tasting substances is a sad way to deprive a toddler of comfort and security that means so much to him, and weaning by 'desertion' (such as going on holiday) will be very stressful for him. If you would like to guide your child's weaning process:

✿ Gradually drop one feed at a time, generally no more than one a week so your child has a chance to adapt to the changes and, if you are breastfeeding, your body will adapt accordingly, so there will be no discomfort with full breasts.

✿ Develop creative alternatives to comforting with the breast or bottle such as a game, a story or a walk to the park. Try to observe your child carefully and stay one step ahead. For instance, if you want to drop an early-morning feed, get up before your child wakes and have a drink and distraction or food ready. Carry snacks and drinks with you when you go out, and if you aren't prepared to nurse your little one for comfort, try not to overextend her so she feels stressed. Let your toddler come to the shops with you to choose her own cup.

✿ Night-time or nap-time feeds are usually the last to go. One simple approach is to gradually substitute story-time: read the same story every night so this becomes the 'bedtime story'. Later on you can read different stories, but 'sameness' helps give little ones a sense of security. You might like to 'overlap' the bedtime feed with another sleep cue. For instance, start playing calming music as you give your child his bedtime feed, then gradually reduce the feed time or the amount of milk in the bedtime bottle and just cuddle with the music playing. Later, you can gradually reduce the volume of the music. Alternatively, your partner could handle the evening routine.

❀ If you are trying to wean a toddler from the breast, try adopting the attitude of 'don't offer, don't refuse'. Toddlers may need to nurse more often when they feel stressed or unwell (it's as though they know they need a boost of antibodies), so please be patient – they will naturally decrease feeds as they recover without any external pressure.

❀ As breastfeeds become spaced further apart, your milk supply decreases and your toddler will become less interested until, one day, painlessly, you may realise that he hasn't asked for a 'booby' for a week or so. He must be weaned!

'My youngest son, Jordan, has just turned three and has weaned and moved into his own room – all in the space of two or three weeks. I have been gently weaning him for a couple of months, not ever saying no, but offering him alternatives, such as a cuddle and a story, milk in a cup, apple 'chippies', sometimes even marshmallows (his favourite!). The last time he was overtired and needed mummy milk I gave it to him. When I asked if there was any milk left, he shook his head and smiled, but remained attached. My one hesitation with weaning him was losing our special cuddle-times but we still have plenty of those.'

Wendy

'Leilani loved the "boobie" – she would have it any time it was offered and any time in between. Every time she fell over in her first two years the boob was the best band-aid! When I became pregnant again I was still feeding her and morning sickness hit me in a big way. I did not feel I had the energy for breastfeeding, growing a baby and keeping up with a two-year-old. I cut back the feeds, and was down to one a day, and because Leilani had a wonderful grasp of language, I decided to do a countdown to total weaning. We counted down the feeds over a period of a week, one to two per day in the last week. We would count on our fingers how many "boobies" to go until they were finished – there was a lot of talking and explaining involved! Of course, when it finished there was a bit of asking for the next few days, but with some more gentle talking, explaining and distracting it worked really well.'

Jessica

Chapter eight
Toilet training

It can be very stressful getting your little one out of nappies and using the potty or toilet. It's a time often made more difficult by judgmental comments from family or neighbours.

Potty time

'All I want is a loo somewhere' could be your theme song if you have a little shadow that follows you everywhere you go, including to the toilet. While private sittings will be a rare luxury for a while yet, there is an upside to sharing the bathroom with your toddler: at this stage in her development your little one learns best from imitation, rather than explanation. Learning how to pee and poo and where to do it is a bit of a mystery to a toddler without a few good role-models. Dad, that includes you too if you have a little fellow.

Helping your toddler to become a competent toilet user

can literally send you 'potty' or it can be an easy-going, child-led process. The key to easy (and less messy) potty training is to wait until your child is emotionally and physically ready. A child who is really ready to go to the loo will know when he needs to go and will be able to tell you this. On the other hand, if you are proudly flashing little Jack's dry jocks as a badge of your 'good mummy toilet-training skills' as you follow him around, juggling the potty, ready to produce it in the nick of time, or you are constantly reminding your toddler, 'It's time to wee,' consider who is really being 'trained' here?

Being able to wee and poo on the potty is a complex process that can't be rushed – your little one needs to be able to recognise when a wee or poo is coming, to hold on long enough to get to the toilet, to remember where the potty is, and to pull down her pants in time to wee without making a puddle. She will also need to be able to understand simple instructions or she won't know what is expected of her or how to tell you she wants to go to the toilet.

'I have let all of my children "train" themselves. That is to say, I offer gentle encouragement but without getting too stressed about it. I let them run around at home with no pants on and

with the potty in easy reach. It's always easier in the warmer weather. My eldest, Alexandra, was toilet trained over the summer the year she turned two (I have some gorgeous photos of her sitting on the potty "reading"). Andrew didn't show any signs of interest or readiness until he was three. Jordan started showing interest in doing wees in the toilet before he was two, but because we were home a lot less (older children's taxi service!) he took a bit longer to be fully toilet trained, but it didn't worry me too much.

'Andrew was in night-time nappies until he was four and a half. One morning he said, "Daddy didn't put a nappy on me last night." I thought, "Oh no, I'll have to go and strip his bed," but before I could say anything he added, "So I got up and weed in the toilet!" Easy as! Like many aspects of parenting, the less one tries to control it, the less one stresses about it, the easier life tends to be.'

Wendy

There are several steps to developing bladder and bowel control:

✿ Your little one will become aware of having a wet or dirty nappy. This will happen sooner if your toddler is in cloth nappies or the newer type of disposable made especially for toddlers that lets him feel wet before the moisture is drawn into the nappy.

✿ She will realise when she is doing a wee or poo – this usually won't happen before about twenty months at the earliest but can take up to two and a half years or even later for some children. You can help your tot learn the words to tell you that she is doing wees and poos (if you haven't already) as you change her nappy.

✿ He can tell you *before* he needs to go. On average, toddlers reach this stage between two and three years.

✿ She can control her urges to go so that she is able to 'hold on' until she gets to the toilet. This tends to happen from about three years onwards.

Signs of readiness

As well as being physically ready to control their bladder and bowels, your child needs to be emotionally ready for toilet learning: regressive stages are normal for toddlers as they work out their place in an ever-changing world and how much they can control it (or not). This can make some little ones want to cling to the security of things they feel comfortable with, and that can include nappies.

If you feel worried that your child is lagging behind,

please be reassured that this isn't a reflection of your child's intelligence or a sign that he is lazy or dirty, any more than it is due to neglect on your part. Toilet readiness is linked to nervous system development and how your child receives and interprets his body's messages. While most children show signs that they are ready for toilet learning by the age of three, at least 15 per cent aren't ready by that age and a small number haven't mastered the process by the age of four years.

Your child is generally physically and emotionally ready for toilet learning when:

- ❀ He asserts his independence in other areas by telling you, 'Me do it!' and 'All by myself!'
- ❀ She can pull her pants up and down.
- ❀ He can sit on a potty without help.
- ❀ She knows what 'wee' and 'poo' are and can tell you.
- ❀ He is curious about what you are doing in the loo (yes, you need to talk about wees and poos, too!)
- ❀ Her nappy is dry for longer periods (at least two hours), showing that she has a good bladder capacity and is developing control.
- ❀ She can follow simple instructions – so she can understand what you want her to do.

✿ He is aware of 'weeing' and 'pooing'. Some little ones get a faraway look as they stop what they are doing to fill their pants; others may wander off into a corner to poo as though they need a little privacy to concentrate.

✿ She may tell you that her nappy is dirty or wet after she has finished and wants it changed. Then (the final step in readiness), when she is aware that she is about to wee or poo *before* it happens, you can explain to her that she can use the potty instead of a nappy.

Even if your toddler is showing signs that he is ready to be encouraged out of nappies, please be mindful that if he is out of sorts or is experiencing a major upheaval such as an illness, moving house, visitors staying or a new baby in the family, or if you are spending Christmas holidays with Grandma and her expensive carpet, it is best for you as well as your child to wait a little longer.

'Jarrah hated nappies from about sixteen months, and would twist and squirm when it came time to put one on. I was pregnant and hated the thought of being kicked in the belly. So I gave up trying to wrestle him and let him roam free at home. I would have a small ice-cream bucket handy so I could catch wees or poos. I became quite good at watching his body

language. After a few months, we got a potty and he took to it
straight away, though he would still miss a few times. Then we
moved house, a new little sister arrived, and hordes of visitors
came around. Despite all this change, he suddenly became
the master of his domain. Now he does everything on the
potty, including reading, drawing and playing cars.'

Natalie

Going to pot

If you have waited until your child is ready, teaching him
to use the potty is really quite simple, in theory at least.
There will be setbacks along the way (so take wipes and
clean clothes when you go out with your newly 'trained'
toddler), but if you take the approach that potty learning
is a bit like any other stage of development, you will get
things into a better perspective when you have a puddle (or
worse). After all, when he learnt to walk, you didn't expect
your child to do this without an occasional trip or fall. And
you didn't scold him if he fell over, did you? Your toddler
isn't being naughty if he wets his pants after managing a
few dry days, so relax and try to see toilet learning in a
similar light. Remember, it won't happen overnight, but it
will happen.

'Aaliyah's a very sensitive child, and even an inadvertent "uh-oh" from Daddy causes her to be so self-conscious that she won't even think about wearing her panties for a week!

'She knows when she needs to go – she runs away and hides. Then she denies she has a poo in her nappy and doesn't want me to change it. It's only when I explain to her that if she leaves it there it will make her bottom and vagina sore, and it could even make her sick, that she'll let me clean it up.

'Then we have the days where she is so excited to wear panties – just like Mummy! And, of course, we have a zillion misses, then eventually she gets it. She sits on the toilet and screams out, "Hip hip, hooray!" a dozen times, throwing her hands in the air. And if she's really excited, she sings happy birthday to herself!

'I have to work on her daddy to be more conscious of what comes out of his mouth, and the effect it has on his precious princess. He is concerned about her "sudden" self-consciousness and is finding it hard to believe it's a natural stage she's going through while she's learning how to control and recognise her body's symptoms.'

Vashti

When your toddler is able to tell you he is wetting or soiling his nappy, suggest, 'You can wee or poo on the potty (or

toilet, if you have a child seat), like Mummy and Daddy.'
You might even like to take him to help you choose a potty.
Be sure to leave the potty where he has easy access to it
and you can keep an eye on him – perhaps in the bathroom
with the door open or in the playroom. And dress your toddler in clothes that are easy to remove.

Buy your little one some fabulous undies – show
them to her and tell her that when she can pee in the toilet she will be really big, then she can wear knickers just
like Mummy or her big siblings (and whoever else seems
impressive to her, but please don't shame her by comparing her to her peers). Then, put the undies in the cupboard
(there is no pressure) until she decides she wants to try
going to the toilet.

Some parents find it helps to show their child what to
do by using a peeing doll or favourite toy to demonstrate;
others simply let their child follow them around – they will
anyway, so you may as well make the most of this and tell
them what you are doing on the toilet.

You may be happy to clear your diary and stay close to
home as you make a concerted, consistent effort at encouraging toilet skills for a week or two, or the very thought of
being stuck at home could send you potty yourself. If staying home and totally focusing isn't your style, you have to

keep to a schedule for older children, or you work all week outside the home, you can take a slightly slower approach by having the potty around (even perhaps taking it out with you) and waiting for your child to lead the way.

If your child is in childcare, discuss what you are doing regarding toilet learning with his carers. They may even have a few good practical tips for you. After all, they will have been through this with lots of other children.

Whether you choose a planned or a more relaxed approach, if you do take your child visiting, please consider others and put pants on her. Although any good friend will forgive a wee accident, it is no fun (and could seriously stretch the friendship!) to clean up after somebody else's child who has been allowed to run around the house making random puddles and deposits that may not be discovered until you have left.

To encourage success that will motivate and excite your child (and you!), time sittings for after a sleep if your toddler wakes up dry. As your toddler relaxes on the potty, their full bladder will release and bingo! A wee in the potty! Also, if they sit on the pot after a meal, there is more likely to be some action. Some parents find it helpful to sit with their child and read a story or sing as they sit on the potty; others offer the child a drink. I never did this as I felt learning to use the toilet was a natural process that 'belonged' to my children as they were ready, so apart from modelling, explaining and being positive, I trusted them to manage it. But if it feels right for you to get more involved in the process, that's your prerogative. The important thing is to stay calm, or your child will pick up on your anxiety.

If at first, your child tells you he needs to use the potty, but his pants are wet – meaning he didn't quite make it – let him sit on the potty and praise him anyway for coming to tell you. He is only a small step away from being dry. Be sure not to make a fuss about misses. As a general rule, don't discuss your child's potty progress in front of him unless you have something positive to say.

Introduce the idea of a toilet as well as a potty (in other people's houses and restaurants, too – and don't worry if your child becomes an 'inspector of loos' for a while, it's a normal fascination). Be aware though that some little ones can be a bit frightened by the toilet at first – after all, it is pretty big for little bums, even with a kiddy seat. You could fall off, or fall in! Also, as you flush, it is slurping up something precious that they have produced. You may not figure out exactly what your toddler is worried about but getting deep and meaningful or dismissing their feelings won't help. On the other hand, oodles of patience and a calm approach on your part will let your toddler see that the big toilet isn't so scary after all. Instead of saying, 'You must be scared or too little' try suggesting, 'You aren't ready yet? Okay, you can use the potty.' Then, 'Now we will pop your poo in the toilet and wave goodbye,' and wave with great pomp and ceremony!

Toddler tactic

To encourage little boys to pee in the toilet, provide a step so he can reach, and pop a ping-pong ball into the loo and get him to squirt the ball!'

Being able to wipe up after wees and poos will take a while yet so although it is okay to teach wiping once your toddler has mastered the art of using the toilet, you will also have to help and supervise (and check for skid marks). Teach your little girl to wipe from front to back so bacteria from the bowel isn't transmitted to her vagina.

When your tot has finished on the loo, make a game of washing hands, singing, 'This is the way we wash our hands, wash our hands.' It will be quite a while, though, before he will do this on his own without reminders or supervision.

Remember, all children are different, so an approach

that works for one child or family won't necessarily feel right for another. The good news is that there doesn't seem to be any evidence that your child will stay in nappies until he is twenty-one or that you will scar him for life because you didn't teach him to use the toilet properly. Having said that, he could (literally!) piss-off a future partner if you don't teach him how to aim and what to do with the toilet seat, but that's a much slower process than learning to keep his pants dry.

'The transition to the toilet progressed quickly and smoothly for our son. The time was right and we followed his lead. He was two just before summer, and I knew from experience with my first-born that it was the perfect time to introduce the idea of not having a nappy! The warmer weather meant that it didn't matter if he ran around naked or in undies for the day. I kept meaning to buy a potty, but I was so busy that summer passed with no progress, and we didn't push the issue. So when it started to get cooler I took Elijah out to choose a potty he liked and explained that it was his special potty for wees.

'He wasn't sure at first but it only took a week and he was onto it – he seemed to prefer to use it in the lounge. There were a couple of accidents in the following weeks, but he really loved his potty – lots of praise and fun was key! He

quickly started recognising when he needed to wee. It took a bit longer for him to feel safe to poo in the potty (he'd ask to have his nappy on to poo and wanted to hide to do it), but it did all happen so quickly. Soon after, he wanted to use it all the time. Dry nappies at night followed a couple of weeks later and coincided with a fascination with the toilet. Now he won't use the potty at all. I couldn't believe how easy it was, but we made it fun and his sister would help us make a fuss over him when he used the potty. He also loved coming with me to flush his wees in the potty in the toilet!'

Kelly

Chapter nine
Caring for tooth, skin and hair

As your little one moves from the (reasonably) compliant baby stage to being a more wilful toddler, you could find that simple tasks like cleaning her teeth, face and hair or even getting her into the bath (once a favourite activity) can become fraught with challenges.

Your toddler's teeth

As well as being necessary for chewing and speaking, healthy baby teeth will help keep spaces for your child's permanent teeth. If your child's baby teeth are healthy, his adult teeth are more likely to grow into their correct position. Besides, you will probably want to avoid the pain (your child's) and expense (yours) of dental work for as long as possible. So now is a good time to teach your toddler healthy dental care habits.

Here are some tips about caring for your toddler's teeth:

✿ Use a soft-bristled infant's toothbrush with a pea-sized dot of junior toothpaste (it has a lower fluoride content) to gently brush all surfaces of your toddler's teeth. Make sure you remove all traces of dried fruit or sweets that can increase the likelihood of tooth decay. Encourage your toddler to spit the toothpaste out rather than swallowing it.

✿ Discourage thumb sucking by ignoring it and distracting your toddler. See he is busy and comfort him with a cuddle when he is tired. Toddlers naturally explore things by tasting and find sucking a comfort. Thumb and finger sucking is normal for many toddlers and it only becomes an issue if it continues beyond toddlerhood when it could push front teeth out of alignment. Be patient, he will eventually give it up.

✿ If your toddler has a dummy, don't *ever* dip it in food or liquids. Sweet substances such as honey or jam will lead to a sweet tooth and decay as they stick around tiny teeth.

✿ If you give your child a bottle at bedtime, only fill it with plain water. When he is asleep, remove the bottle – during sleep, less saliva is produced to wash away acids and protect teeth. Milk, fruit juice or sweetened liquids that drip from a bottle into a toddler's mouth after he has dozed off may pool against his teeth and cause decay.

❀ Encourage your child to drink plain water during the day as well – she doesn't need cordial or fruit juice – and take care to read labels for 'hidden' sugars: glucose, sucrose, fructose and honey are all sweets.

Toddler tactic: make teeth-cleaning fun

Tooth brushing is an important routine that needs to be done at least twice a day. The difficult part is getting your toddler to cooperate. It is ideal to start teeth-cleaning as soon as the first teeth emerge but if your efforts have been a bit hit and miss you can encourage your tot by making it fun:

❀ *Choose a toothbrush with a little animal or cartoon face on the handle – the battery-operated ones can be fun for two- and three-year-olds, who can choose their own toothbrush.*

❀ *Use two toothbrushes – one for you and one for your toddler – to stop him trying to wrench 'his' brush away when it's your turn to brush (so you can make sure they are done properly).*

❀ *Give him a decorated plastic glass for rinsing.*

❀ *Use toothpaste that your child likes the taste of – a fruity one may be preferable to a minty taste.*

❀ *Brush your teeth at the same time your child brushes her* teeth, so that she can copy you. It could be fun to get your own cartoon brush, just like hers!

❀ Encourage your toddler to 'open wide' by sitting him in front of a mirror so he can watch you cleaning his teeth.

❀ Teach him to brush up and down – cleaning sideways won't get the bits out between his teeth and may make his gums sore.

❀ Sing a teeth-cleaning song. Try the tune of 'Row, row, row your boat' with the words, 'Clean, clean, clean your teeth, gently all around, merrily, merrily, merrily, smiley up and down.'

First dental visits

Unless your child has obvious problems, a good time to begin dental visits is at about two years. Then your dentist can pick up any signs of trouble early. Try to find a dentist who specialises in treating children or one who simply has a good rapport with kids.

To encourage a positive attitude to dental visits:

❀ Take your child along when you go for a dental check-up yourself. This will pave the way for questions and discussion, and perhaps the handling of a few implements such as a 'tooth mirror' or a ride in the chair.

✤ Keep discussion about the dentist positive: don't frighten your toddler by telling her, 'If you don't let me brush your teeth, you will have to go to the dentist and get them drilled.'

✤ Avoid using negative words when you talk about the dentist. Steer clear of words like drill, needle and hurt, and when you do take your child to the dentist please don't tell him to 'be brave' or 'this won't hurt'. Most kiddy dental treatments are pretty straightforward so there is no need to create unnecessary fear by making inappropriate suggestions.

✤ Make your toddler's dental appointment early in the day, so that tiredness doesn't result in uncooperative behaviour.

Bath time

Most little ones love water, but sometimes even water-babies resist bath time. This can often happen around arsenic hour – that early-evening time when his blood sugar and your tolerance levels are low. So, how do you convince a toddler to take a bath, especially when he is tired and cranky?

The simple answer, whatever time of day you want to

bath your toddler, is to try to make bath time fun. Here are some suggestions:

❀ If you have to interrupt a game to get your child moving towards his bath-time routine, take him a snack. As well as creating a diversion, this will address the low blood sugar. Then announce, 'I am running your bath.' Your tot will have a few minutes to get used to the idea and move along.

❀ Pretend there are fairies in your bathroom. If there is fairy dust around the bathtub your toddler might believe you. Sprinkle some glitter around the rim of the bath when you are filling the tub, then call your little one in to look for the fairies.

❀ A magic coloured bath can encourage children to get down and dirt-free. Add a few drops of food colouring to the water. If you need to bath two kids together, you can be sure they will each choose different colours. No problem! Let them watch as Sarah's red colour mixes with Jack's yellow colour and see what happens.

❀ Let your little ones body paint with coloured shaving foam (add a few drops of food colour to the shaving foam). You can also buy bath crayons for drawing on little bodies in the bath – it simply washes off!

✿ Although there are some great and inexpensive bath toys, you don't need them to entice your child to have fun in the tub. Empty plastic bottles, squirty bottles, bubbles, sponges and wooden blocks (do they sink or float? Are they sailing boats?) can be just as entertaining and educational.

✿ If you want to conserve water, why not take a bath or shower with your little rascal? And remember to promptly empty any buckets that you may use to collect water for recycling – toddlers are top-heavy, and can drown if they overbalance head-first into a bucket of water.

✿ For safety's sake, always supervise your child in the bath, even a shallow bath. Tricky tots can climb and slip in a split second, especially in a slippery bath. If your child does take a dipping and becomes frightened in the bath, get in with him next time to show him it really is safe and fun.

Washing your toddler's hair

Hair-washing is one job that can be made easier with a few simple tricks:

✿ Encourage your child to let you hold him lying back

while you wash his hair. The soapy water will run down behind him, rather than into his eyes.

✿ Make hair-washing a family thing – one parent can tip your child back (make it a game) while the other rinses shampoo off.

✿ Try using a shampoo shade to protect his eyes as you wash your little one's hair.

✿ Use a baby shampoo that doesn't sting. An all-in-one shampoo and conditioner will make the process quicker.

✿ If your toddler is reluctant to be held, encourage him to lie on his back and 'float' the water off his hair: get him to cover his eyes with a folded face washer while you quickly rinse.

✿ Rinse off shampoo with clean water (at least for the final rinse), not water containing bath soap as it could irritate your little one's scalp.

Toddler tactic: removing cradle cap

If your toddler has a dry scalp or cradle cap (which appears as an oily crust), massage his scalp with olive oil and leave it in overnight. Wash his hair in the morning with a mild shampoo and most of the dry skin will lift off – without you picking at his scalp, which will hurt and may become infected.

Chapter ten
Goodnight, sleep tight

Just as there is a wide variation in other aspects of normal toddler development, there can be quite a difference in sleeping patterns, too. Like adults, children have varying sleep requirements – some may sleep through the night and also have an afternoon nap until they are school age, while other tots survive on much less sleep than their parents would like!

If you feel like the only parent who still has a little night howl on your hands (or who sneaks into your bed at 3 a.m.), take heart. With patience and a few sensible strategies, you will be able to create a healthy sleep environment that also respects your toddler's developmental needs.

The wakeful toddler

Reasons for night waking can be unique for each child and it can often take a bit of detective work to pinpoint the causes. But be reassured, it isn't your fault or your child's (he is not 'naughty' and you are not an incompetent parent!) that your little one wakes and needs reassurance in the night. Toddler sleep can be affected by developmental stages, discomfort or bad dreams.

Developmental stages

Despite the varied reasons for night waking, there is a common thread around waking and bedtime behaviour when we consider developmental stages.

From twelve to eighteen months

A lot of parents become quite disheartened about their toddler's waking at this age. They feel they have followed the baby's lead for a whole year (or more!) and there seems no sign that this child will ever sleep through the night. Often this brings dissent between partners as one exerts pressure to 'make that child sleep' and the other loses faith that the toddler will ever sleep without desperate measures such as shutting the bedroom door and leaving their child to cry himself to sleep.

In fact, this is a disastrous age to leave little ones to cry it out, as separation anxiety is at a peak at about twelve months, and after all the work you have done teaching your baby to trust you, the light is just around the corner (honestly!), even if you do nothing at all but continue to respond to your baby with love. If you are exhausted and fractious, and feel a need to do something, you can make changes sensitively without leaving your child to scream. It is best to work with your partner to make a plan of action if changes are in order.

At bedtime, your toddler's separation anxiety could mean that for a while he may want only one parent, usually the primary carer, to put him to bed. It is fine to go along with this, with the other parent involved in part of the pre-bedtime ritual such as bathing or massage (if this works for your family), and gradually increasing their involvement. As your toddler's separation anxiety eases, the other parent can try settling him.

You may also need to sit in your toddler's room (perhaps with a hand on him) as he falls asleep. Don't try to force him to self-settle before he is ready as bedtime should never be associated with fear. Some parents find that giving their toddler a transitional object such as a soft toy can be a comfort. If you do this, try to avoid using the comfort object as a substitute for your attention. Also, plan to have two or three of the same objects in case one gets misplaced and alternate these so they all have the same smell, otherwise the new object may be rejected.

About now, many toddlers will start to drop a daytime sleep, so that soon they will be having just one sleep during the day. Dropping sleeps can be tricky: you still want your baby in bed at a reasonable time but sometimes she will need an extra sleep late in the afternoon (or may fall asleep in the car, for instance) and this may make bedtime later some nights. If your child is still having two daytime naps at this stage or she goes to bed very early, you may be able to 'tweak' her day sleeps so she drops down to one afternoon nap, or move her bedtime gradually later and see if this makes a difference.

If you want to change your baby's sleep times (either for day or night sleeps) you will need to do it gradually, by fifteen-minute increments every few days, rather than an hour all at once. This means moving bedtime either earlier or later, depending on what you are trying to achieve, from fifteen minutes for a few days to half an hour and so on. If you decide you want your child in bed an hour earlier and suddenly spring this upon her, you are likely to have an hour of battling on your hands until her little body clock is ready to allow her to sleep. It really isn't efficient to start bedtime battles because you want a quick fix as this isn't likely to be the result.

From eighteen months on

As your toddler becomes more mobile, life is often far too exciting to interrupt by going to bed – at least that seems to be the lively child's perspective! This is when a predictable rhythm to the day and a gentle wind-down ritual before bed becomes vital to help your child 'switch off'. Try to finish boisterous games early in the evening, turn off the television and create a calm atmosphere before bed. Increased comprehension and language skills will make bedtime gradually easier as story-time becomes a welcome part of the evening.

Many parents tell me that after close, hands-on bedtime parenting, they feel confident that little ones between 18 months and two years are ready for some limit-setting around bedtimes. Possibly because the child's needs have been so well met, changes can be made fairly easily without any distress to the child or angst for the parents. It is important that changes such as night weaning are made carefully in response to your child's needs, not because of outside pressures from friends or relatives. For more information about making changes slowly, please read my book *Sleeping Like a Baby*. Also, be reassured that even if you don't set any strict limits for your toddler, all children eventually learn to sleep through the night without your help to resettle.

'Jed was always a great sleeper. After the newborn phase, he only ever woke once a night for a breastfeed and settled down quickly afterwards. At seven and a half months, he started to sleep through the night. This lasted until he was about twelve months old, then he started waking for a feed in the night again. This time, when Jed woke, I'd bring him into my bed, and feed him lying down while I snoozed. If I woke later and he was asleep, I'd put him back in his cot.

'As he passed eighteen months of age, the waking started to become more frequent. He was relying more on the comfort of the night feeds. Now he was waking once at about 11 p.m., so I would feed him and then put him back in his cot. Then he'd usually wake again at about 2 a.m. He wasn't a good bed partner – he kicked and moved around a lot.

'I decided that I wanted to night wean him. When he woke at 11 p.m., I would pick him up, explain that it was night time, that he could have milk in the morning and rock and sing to resettle. He would usually yell, "Milk! Milk!" for the first few minutes, and wriggle and stiffen in my arms, then he'd usually relax and settle down. After ten minutes he was asleep and I was able to put him in his cot. Then he'd wake again at 2 a.m. So in I'd go to do the same thing, and eventually he'd settle. It probably took about fifteen minutes all up, but this felt like ages in the middle of the night, especially when I knew it would *have been very easy to take him into bed with me.*

'*I did this for about three to four nights in a row and sud-denly he started sleeping all the way through. If he did wake, he wasn't calling out or shaking the cot. I even found that he didn't wake as easily when the television was too loud, or someone laughed loudly in the evenings. At two and a half, he still loves his breastfeed in the mornings, and so do I. It's very relaxing and buys me at least another forty-five minutes in bed!*'

Simone

Two to three years

Delaying bedtime becomes an art at this stage. These little people like to be where the action is and they seem to have no idea that they aren't miniature adults. They can also feel stressed about incidents that have happened during their busy day. The good news is that your active, wriggly toddler will enjoy snuggling and listening to a bedtime story and, generally closer to three years, a meditation is a sure way to help him drift off, relaxed and with pleasant dreams. (See Meditation, page 253.) Your calm presence and physical contact at bedtime will activate brain chemicals that reduce your toddler's anxiety and encourage him to sleep.

'I was worried about how I'd get Hugo to have his afternoon sleeps when Isobel arrived (Hugo was just over two years old). The week after her birth, we had so many people in our house that Hugo's sleep patterns were completely thrown. Once everything returned to normal, and it was just me and the kids, I thought I'd have trouble getting him to sleep. But after lunch we'd go to our bed and I'd read Hugo two stories. If Isobel was already asleep, she'd be on the bed with us. If not, I'd breast-feed her while lying down and reading Hugo stories. When the books were read, I'd just hold Hugo's hand (Isobel was usually between us) and he'd go to sleep. It was lovely to have afternoon sleeps in bed together! I made sure no matter what we did in the morning, we'd be back home for the three of us to sleep in the afternoon.'

Joanne

Your toddler's delaying tactics at bedtime – needing a drink, one more kiss, a lost toy – are her way of saying, 'I really want you to stay with me.' From a toddler's perspective, it may be difficult to relax and fall asleep if she feels stressed about being left in her room alone, especially if she can hear adults having fun (talking, watching television) in another part of the house. Consider, also, if this is the only time of her day that your little one has your undivided attention. If this is the case, try to spend more one-on-one time with her during the day so her needs aren't so intense at bedtime.

A consistent bedtime routine with specific rituals is important to enlist your toddler's cooperation and help him feel secure. If your child seems especially clingy at bedtime, try telling him the story of his day so that he can process the emotional ups and downs and let them go.

Once your toddler is closer to three, you can begin setting limits at bedtime by telling him how many stories you will read before you start. To minimise delaying tactics and calling out, try to anticipate his needs: before he gets into bed, let him get his toys in order and perhaps choose a soft toy to sleep with; place a lidded cup of water within his reach; before you settle down to read, ask him, 'What is the one last thing you need to do before stories?' Help your child stay in bed until he is sleepy by sitting in his room with him.

One lovely ritual is to lead your toddler through a relaxation exercise by quietly saying goodnight to each of her body parts and telling her to feel them becoming heavy and sleepy. Start at the toes, move to the legs, knees, tummy and so on, up to, 'Goodnight, sleepy eyes.' If she talks, remind her in a quiet, calm voice that it is sleep time. If you have things you need to do or you are moving to the next stage of helping your child get to sleep by herself, you could tell her that you will check on her in five minutes. It is important to keep this promise so that she relaxes, knowing you will be back soon. As you check on her, give her a kiss and leave again for another five minutes. If she gets up, try not to yell or you will wake her even more. Simply take her by the hand, lead her back to bed and tuck her in. Then, in a calm voice, tell her you will check on her in five minutes (or sit with her until she is settled before leaving her for the next five-minute period). She will probably need to be close to three years or older before this will work, at least most of the time. At any time of increased stress, a child of any age can be helped by extra support at bedtime.

'When I could no longer lie down with my three-year-old, I would say, "Lie down in my bed," (always more special) and "I'll check on you." I would then check on her thirty seconds later and say, "See, I told you I'd come and check," and then come in again in one minute, and so on, till she fell asleep. If she wanted to talk I'd tell her it was sleep time and that I'd keep checking as long as she lay still and cuddled her toy/ blankey/whatever . . . This reassured her that I wasn't far away and would always come if she called out.'

Kate

Toddler tactic: encourage independent sleep

To wean your toddler off needing your presence at bedtime, a fun game to help her settle is 'hunt the teddies'. When it is almost bedtime, prepare your child's bedroom – dim the lights and warm her bed with a wheat pack if it's a cool night (but remove it when she hops into bed so she can't burn herself). Then, hide your child's teddies around the house. Ask her to help you find them so she can put them all to bed. When she finds the teddies say, 'The teddies look very tired. Can you help them go to sleep?' Tuck the teddies into bed with her and ask her to help them settle down and go to sleep. They will need lots of cuddles! Chances are, your caring little toddler will drift off as she snuggles her teddies to sleep.

Discomfort

Could your child have difficulty settling to sleep because she is uncomfortable? Is she too hot or too cold? An ideal room temperature is between 16 and 20 degrees Celsius. Could her feet be cold? Consider how difficult it is to sleep with cold feet and put slippers or socks on her before bed. If your child is a restless sleeper who kicks off blankets, a sleeping bag will keep her warm during the night as the air cools down.

Are her pyjamas roomy enough that they don't pull or

rise up as she wriggles around? Are there tags that could scratch or tickle? Use a low-irritant detergent to prevent 'itching' and buy pyjamas made from natural fabrics rather than a synthetic blend.

Lie in your toddler's bed (or where her cot stands) at night to see how comfortable the space where she sleeps is. Can you feel draughts from a window? (Don't ever place a child's bed within reach of blind or curtain cords and lock windows.) Are lights shining in from the street, the hallway or other rooms? Do lights shine into your child's eyes or do they create shadows that could be scary?

If you look at your child's sleep environment from her perspective, you will be able to change it so that it is comfortable and encourages sleep.

Bad dreams

If your child wakes from a scary dream, respect her fears – they are real to her. Hold her and reassure her, 'I am here, you are safe.' Stay as long as she needs you. During the day, when she is more likely to be rational, you could tell her, 'When I was little I used to have scary dreams too but I learned to change the end of dreams so they weren't scary any more.'

Help her think of ways to beat the scary creatures she

dreams about. For instance, try creating a special sound that makes snakes disappear or using a spray that evaporates monsters or makes them into friendly monsters (put a few drops of lavender essential oil into a spray bottle of water and spray this around her room). A nightlight (you can call this the good fairy light) or a dream-catcher hung above your child's bed may help her feel more confident about going to sleep. Also, consider the role television can play in creating frightening images – for an easier transition to bed and better sleep, it is best to keep the television switched off after dinner until your child is in bed.

Waking early

Typically, toddlers are ready to wake as soon as the first ray of sunshine hits the window, and this can be more pronounced as they reach new developmental milestones (such as starting to walk). Blackout blinds or heavy, dark-coloured curtains may help extend your toddler's morning wake-up time. A sippy cup of water and a few safe toys or board books put next to the bed or cot the night before may buy you a few extra minutes if your child will amuse himself for a while when he wakes. If noise from the street or from other family members is waking your toddler, you could set a clock radio on a station that plays classical music or between stations so it plays white noise. If it starts to play before your child would normally wake, this might help him sleep through the early-morning sounds.

If your toddler goes to bed early and has a good sleep but wakes early, he is probably waking because he has had sufficient sleep. You can either try gradually adjusting his bedtime at night (move bedtime later by ten to fifteen minutes every few nights) and hope that he will sleep a little later in the morning or 'wear it'. Either have an extra cuddle in bed with your toddler or get up and have fun as you greet the day together – I am talking to you, dads!

Food and sleep

Your toddler's sleep patterns can be affected by his diet. Night waking can be caused by allergies or food intolerance. In one study at a UK sleep clinic, 12 per cent of thirteen-month-old infants who presented with persistent night waking for which no other causes were found were taken off all milk products when cow's milk intolerance was suspected. In most of these children, sleep normalised within five weeks, with night-time awakenings falling to nil or once per night. A subsequent milk 'challenge', in which neither the subjects nor the researchers knew who'd had milk and who'd had the placebo, induced the reappearance of insomnia and, after a year, when the challenge was repeated, all but one child reacted with wakeful behaviour again.

Although not every child will respond to milk and other dairy products with sleep difficulties, if you suspect an allergy may be the reason for your child's wakefulness, you can try eliminating a particular food for a couple of weeks and see if it makes a difference. Before you make any drastic alterations to your child's diet, it is sensible to check with your doctor and ask for a referral to a dietician who specialises in allergies and working with children.

Restless sleep can also be related to sensitivity to additives in processed foods and soft drinks. Please don't ever give your toddler any drink that contains caffeine (Coke, Diet Coke, iced tea, hot chocolate) or guarana – day or night! This will hype-up behaviour and prevent your child from being able to sleep well, if at all. Some sensitive children may be affected by naturally occurring chemicals such as salicylates in otherwise healthy foods like grapes, oranges, strawberries or tomatoes, and, as well as causing behaviour changes, these can affect sleep.

As I mentioned in chapter 7 (page 191), tracking down

offending foods can take some detective work, and if food allergies are suspected, you may need to eliminate foods for at least ten days to see whether this has any positive effects. Rather than becoming stressed over food (as well as your child's sleep), it could help to simply reduce the amount or combination of foods. So, instead of giving your child grapes and strawberries for dessert after a spaghetti with tomato sauce dinner, just try these foods separately in smaller amounts.

Some foods may actually aid sleep. For instance, essential fatty acids (EFAs) are vital nutrients for infants' and toddlers' developing brains. Research is showing that low levels of DHA, an omega-3 fatty acid, may contribute to behavioural and learning difficulties as well as poor sleep patterns. It is relatively simple to add these nutrients to your child's diet – although you can buy appropriate supplements for children (ask your doctor, pharmacist or naturopath), the best sources are oily fish such as salmon, tuna and sardines. If you are a vegetarian or have a toddler who won't eat fish, you can use cold-pressed linseed or flaxseed oil on salads or in smoothies (cooking will destroy the nutrients). Eating greens can also have an effect on sleep. Although no self-respecting tot is likely to wolf down green veggies in large amounts, it is worth noting that nature's relaxant – magnesium – is found in high quantities in green leafy vegetables.

Bedtime snacks may also affect sleep, either positively or negatively. For instance, high-protein foods can trigger the production of dopamine, a hormone that will keep your child aroused, while a banana will help boost tryptophan levels, the substance needed to make the mood-stabilising (calming) chemical serotonin that will encourage sound sleep. If you want to keep up with your child during the day, boost your own energy levels with protein snacks throughout the day.

Time for bed

Falling asleep, especially at night time, is a major transition for little ones. If they sleep alone, they are leaving you, temporarily. At various developmental stages, this may be stressful to your toddler, so she will cling to the security of the person she loves the most in the whole big world – you! Implementing a predictable bedtime rhythm can help children feel secure and will allow them to relax into sleep more easily. Also, your presence at bedtime helps regulate and prime children's physiology for sleep. For instance, a story will engage the frontal lobe of your child's brain and this will inhibit motor impulses. If you read or tell a story in a dimmed light, the semi-darkness will help her release melatonin, a hormone that induces sleep. A bedtime cuddle will activate opioids and the hormone oxytocin which combine to create a naturally calming effect on your child's brain, helping her shift into a sleepy state.

Rather than seeing settling your toddler as a negative sleep association, or worrying that she will never become 'independent', appreciate the benefits of sharing this precious time. Over years of observation, I have noticed that children who are parented to sleep as babies and toddlers are far more likely to view sleep as a warm and comforting experience and actually enjoy bedtime. As your child develops language skills, a bedtime routine can include stories and talks about your child's day. The trust that builds as your child confides in you is not something to be dismissed as an inconvenience to your busy life, but a foundation for an ongoing relationship. When your child is school-aged, you will get all the 'gossip' at bedtime, you will know what worries as well as what motivates your child, and when things aren't going well you will be able to step in because you will be attuned and present.

The ultimate goal is to impart the skills your child needs to fall asleep without you (most of the time) but there is no hurry and, in fact, if your toddler senses your stress or urgency, this could backfire. If he goes to sleep feeling anxious or cries himself to sleep, he is unlikely to sleep well due to the stress hormones that are activated in his brain from being left to cry. He may also wake more during the night or he may express feelings of insecurity by becoming clingy during the day.

On the other hand, a child who feels secure about sleep time is likely to become more independent in the long term. It seems a more logical choice to calm and connect with your little one at bedtime and create a positive sleep environment, than to create bedtime battles or anxiety around sleep that may last beyond infancy.

'While we were on holiday, we taught Hugo to sleep without feeding. It turned out to be much easier than I expected. Simon (his dad) and Hugo would head to the beach every morning straight after brekky. After playing and running around, Hugo would be tuckered out when they came in at about 10 a.m. He'd have something to eat and drink, we'd lie down with him and read him stories and he'd fall asleep. It sometimes took about thirty minutes, but it worked!'

Joanne

Bedtime routines

Toddlers can be very pedantic about the order of their bedtime routine and will even insist on kissing their toys goodnight in a specific order. This is not a sign that your child is becoming obsessive – he will grow out of this, but for now, a predictable bedtime routine can help him feel secure and in control as his accelerating development creates changes for him every day. Just a word of caution, however: it pays to keep bedtime fairly simple so that if you leave your child with a babysitter, the routine can be duplicated. Your child's bedtime routine can include: bathing, massage, songs, stories or meditation, or a combination of any of these elements, depending on your toddler's age.

Bathing

The relaxing effects of a bath work at a physiological level as well as a psychological one. One of the triggers for sleep is a slight drop in core body temperature. A warm bath temporarily increases the core body temperature, then as this temperature lowers after a bath, we feel drowsy – this is why timing of the bath matters. It is best to have a quiet play before your child's bath, then dress her warmly and take her to bed, drowsy from the bath, for the remainder of her bedtime routine.

A few drops of lavender mixed with vegetable oil or milk or a baby bath product that incorporates essential oils can be added to the bathwater for extra soothing effects. Be careful, though, about using bubble bath. Read labels carefully and use all bath additives sparingly as these can cause dry, itching skin and genital tract irritation that may cause your toddler great discomfort and keep her awake at night.

Bathing with your toddler can be a special fun and bonding time for you both, or, if you prefer, you could take a shower together.

Massage

If you can get your wriggly toddler to keep still long enough to allow you to massage him, silent nights could be at your fingertips. Research from Miami University shows that infants and toddlers who were massaged daily for one month, for fifteen minutes prior to bedtime, fell asleep more easily than they had prior to the study. Massage releases endorphins, those 'feel good' hormones that help us all reduce stress. With fewer stress hormones circulating in his body, your toddler will inevitably sleep more soundly.

Unless you have introduced massage to your child as a baby, it is unlikely that he will keep still long enough to relax and enjoy a massage as a one-year-old. Even then, as the rage to run takes over, your baby who once enjoyed massage may not be still long enough to massage at bedtime. If this is the case, try massaging his hands, feet and legs or make some gentle circles on his back during the day if and when he is happy to have a little rub. Try for a longer massage in a few weeks (or months). Then, when he is happy to be massaged and associates this with relaxation, you can introduce massage as a bedtime ritual. Remember, though, to always ask your child's permission to massage him and respect his response. This way you are teaching him that his body is his own and that he has a right to refuse any unwanted touching.

Often, rather than a 'formal' massage, simply stroking your child's forehead or rubbing his hands or back when he is lying in bed can help him 'wind down' and relax. But if you'd like to learn some massage techniques, see Pizza massage, page 136.

Songs

Singing a 'sleepy song' to your child at bedtime will help him relax and it is a very portable ritual that you can use anywhere, any time. If you use recorded music, it is worth making a few copies of the CD so you can take one with you if you go on holiday. If your toddler is wakeful and you can't find a specific reason (such as being too hot or cold, thirsty or uncomfortable), a song may help him settle. You may like to switch the CD onto continuous play so music is on a low volume throughout the night.

Stories

Even if you love reading and are happy to read several stories at bedtime, it is good to use the same story as the 'sleepy story'. Many toddlers love listening to a combination of *Where is the Green Sheep?* followed by *Time for Bed*, both by Mem Fox. As you read to your child, the calming effects are increased if you cuddle up together – the body contact will encourage your child to release oxytocin, which reduces stress hormones such as cortisol.

Little ones vary in their ability to listen and engage in stories. **One-year-olds** generally enjoy stories about familiar objects and people or animals. They like to hear you talk about these rather than listen to a 'proper' story being read. They also like tactile books and want to point to pictures as you talk about them.

Two-year-olds will enjoy being read short stories and have favourite books that they like to read over and over. A favourite story can become the 'bedtime' book.

Even active **three-year-olds** will sit through a story or ten! And, heaven help you if you get a word wrong or try to hurry things along by skipping a page. It helps to be consistent about how many stories you are prepared to read at bedtime so your child isn't confused about what to expect if one night you are happy to read ten stories but another you will only read one.

> ### Toddler tactic: use your voice
> *Save your fabulous, expressive reading voice for daytime, or at least become less and less animated as you read at bedtime. Reading in a calm, quiet voice will help her settle, as opposed to razzing her up!*

Meditation

We are constantly hearing about the benefits of meditation for adults: studies show that regular meditation can lower blood pressure and relieve anxiety and stress. So by doing a bedtime meditation with your toddler, you will be warding off the evils of your own stressful life as you soothe your child into dreamtime.

Meditation is a simple way to help your active child, from about three years old or perhaps slightly younger, to be still and drift off to sleep. To lead your child gently to sleep through meditation, try these steps.

❀ Calm yourself by breathing in and out slowly. You can get your child to do this with you by asking him to close his eyes and feel the cool air as he breathes in and the warm air as he breathes out. You can count each breath if you like.

❀ Begin the meditation by asking your child to imagine a star in his mind. Then ask him to visualise a colour for the star, which shines down on him 'warming' his head and then spreading down through his body to his toes as you name each body part in turn. This is called a guided relaxation.

❀ Next, ask your child to feel his heart filling with love for people, animals or creatures (whatever seems appropriate). Then ask him to picture his guardian angel wrapping protective golden wings around him and leading him to the 'worry tree' where he pins all his worries. Pause a few seconds to allow your child to focus on the big tree and release any difficulties he may have had during the day, or you could gently give words to help express these.

❀ Then take your child through the gate into his 'magic garden', and once he is 'inside' lead him into a story. The length of the story and the meditation depends on your child's state of relaxation. For instance, he may walk down the garden path to the water's edge and watch or play with dolphins in the water, he may follow a bunny rabbit through the garden to his burrow where he could eat carrots for dinner with the bunny family, or he may find a circus, or fairies – whatever your little one is into.

❀ Take your time and be creative, keeping your voice slow and calm as opposed to expressive and exciting. Ideally, you will become as relaxed as your child who will drift off, snug in his bed, ready for sweet dreams.

❀ You can do a simple version of guided relaxation with a younger tot by asking her to close her eyes as you say (in a slow, calm voice), 'Goodnight sleepy feet, goodnight sleepy legs, knees, tummy . . .' and so on up to sleepy eyes.

A room of their own

Your toddler may already have a bedroom of his own, but if he is still sleeping in a family bed or in your room, you are probably wondering when and how to move him to his own space. Or, if he is in a cot in his room, you may be considering when to make the move to a big bed.

The simple answer is to make changes when life is fairly stable for your family. It isn't easy to change sleeping arrangements if there is already major upheaval such as a new baby, a new house or if your toddler has just started childcare. If you are expecting another baby, it is best to make changes well in advance. For instance, if you will need the cot for your new baby, you don't want your toddler feeling that he has been pushed out of his bed by a little intruder so either make (or trial) changes well before baby arrives. If your toddler is likely to be in his cot for another year or so, perhaps you need to get another cot for the baby. Or, if he sleeps well it might be time to try a bed. You can always try a new sleep situation and see whether it works, then go back to the cot for a while longer if your toddler starts wandering or has other problems in a bed.

Perhaps the best indicator of when your child is ready to move from cot to bed is when he is able to 'escape' from his cot. Climbing out of a low bed is obviously much safer then falling from a cot. Also, if your toddler is using the toilet it will be easier to take him to the loo (or for him to take himself) if he is sleeping in a bed.

The answer to 'how' to make changes is gradually, with love. If, for instance, your toddler has been sleeping in your bed, depending on his age and readiness, you could move him to a cot or bed in your room. At first put his cot or bed next to your bed, then move it to the other side of the room, then eventually to his own room. Whether you are moving your toddler into his own room or from cot to bed, it will help to enlist your child's help to set up his bedroom, perhaps taking him to choose bedding or getting him to draw a picture for his room. Allow him to play in his room and become familiar with it before making night-time moves, then start with day sleeps in the new bed. He may be happy to sleep there at night fairly quickly or this could be a more gradual process.

If you make your child's room a sanctuary that he asso-ciates with pleasant feelings, rather than a place where he feels abandoned or alone (don't send him to his room as a punishment), and if changes are made gradually and sen-sitively, there will be fewer struggles around sleep time and the transition will happen more 'permanently'. However, at times of stress, you can expect some regressive behaviour and this may mean your toddler wanders into your room or bed for some night-time comfort. At night, your child can't see well so he will rely on his senses of touch and smell to feel safe. This is why it is natural for him to seek your presence if he wakes and feels frightened, concerned or disorientated.

'For a little over two years, our son Cooper either slept in our bed or had his cot in our room. When we moved his cot to another room, he would spend most of the night in there but when he woke he ended up in our bed. This was mostly fine except on occasion we would end up in the H formation with Travis and I lying side by side with Cooper making the rest of the H between us. We talked about transferring Cooper into his own bed after we worked out that he was waking because he was hitting his head on the side of the cot. Also, I think we were waking him up when we went to bed ourselves. I purchased some bed linen and a safety rail for the side to prevent Cooper from falling out. When I was setting up the bed I made sure he was with us and explained to him that he was to sleep in his special bed all night.

'After a couple of nights, he started sleeping through and basically did so for several months. I was pregnant with our second child at the time so knew that any change had to be made well before the baby arrived. Towards the end of my pregnancy, Cooper did become more wakeful as I think he knew something major was about to change in his life and he sought some extra attention.

'Now, when Cooper does wake, Travis is able to resettle him and often ends up falling asleep in the bed with him. Usually at around 6.30 a.m. Cooper ends up back in our bed for early-morning cuddles as he is able to get out of the bed himself.'

Helen

'Hugo had been sleeping in his own room for a few months before our baby was born. But when Isobel came along, Hugo would wake every time she cried during the night. As Isobel got jaundice and wouldn't breastfeed, her feeds (especially at night) were pretty full-on. I would express, Simon would feed her via a syringe, and we'd have Hugo awake and jumping on the bed as well! After two nights of this, we placed the old cot mattress on the floor beside our bed and Hugo slept there. He would stir when Isobel woke up, lift his head, decide it was all pretty boring, and would roll over and sleep again. He stayed in our room for the first three to four months of Isobel's life, then moved back to his room. Isobel is now eight months old and Hugo is a frequent night visitor. We still have the mattress on the floor and if he wakes up during the night, he'll come into our room and sleep there.'

Joanne

Chapter eleven
Another baby

You may already have another child, or you may be contemplating when would be the best time to add to your family. This is a very personal decision and there are pros and cons however you choose to space your children. Small children close in age may take up an enormous amount of your physical energy, but later they may be good playmates (or not). You will be through the exhausting baby stage a little more quickly if your children are closely spaced, but you are kidding yourself if you think that having babies close together means you will be done with the hard yards when they can walk, talk, start school or whatever. Being a parent means at least eighteen years of considering your child's needs as (or even before) you meet your own, whatever the age gaps. One upside of having larger gaps between children is that you may feel able to give each child more individual attention, especially when they are babies.

A high-need baby may scare you off having babies close in age while a placid baby could see you thinking you could do this again, real soon! Just beware though, if you are feeling smug about how wonderful your first child is, this could be as much due to your child's good nature as your good management. There's no guarantee your second baby will be the same. You could find a second baby much more than you (or your toddler) bargained for if you happen to get a higher-needs baby, or if your easy-going first baby turns into a daredevil toddler.

> *'When I had my first child, a friend's mum sat me down and told me to ignore everyone's comments about child spacing. She said that children will get along or they won't: it doesn't matter if it's a one-year, three-year or eight-year gap. She said a little bit of that is parenting, but mostly you have no control over it. She said the perfect gap was when I was ready, and that I shouldn't let anyone tell me any different. It was advice I cherished and heeded, waiting until my husband and I were both ready before we planned baby number two.'*
>
> **Kate**

Preparing your toddler for a new baby

Bonding with a new sibling can begin well before the baby is born and may well avert some rivalry issues. How soon you explain to your toddler that you are having a baby is your own choice but do remember that hearing from people outside the family can confuse your child and may make him feel excluded. For toddlers, who have a very limited sense of time, it is best to link the birth to an event they do understand such as 'after Christmas', 'before your birthday' or 'around the time we have our Easter eggs'. Meanwhile, sharing your pregnancy with your older child or children can aid understanding of this miraculous process and will encourage bonding.

Here are some things that may help:

✿ Encourage your toddler to 'cuddle' the baby, talk and sing to it, and feel it moving, perhaps guessing which body part is wriggling. (Do you think that is a foot or a hand, or is it his bottom?)
✿ Allow your toddler to join in prenatal exercises or yoga.
✿ Role-play with dolls to stimulate discussion about birth and the needs of a newborn. For example, 'When you were a baby . . .', 'The baby will be too little to eat food like you so he will drink milk from Mummy's breasts just like you used to.'
✿ Take your child to visit a friend with a newborn for a close-up look.

❀ Look at picture books that show the various stages of in utero development and say things like, 'Our baby is this big now,' or 'Look, now our baby will be growing fingernails.'

❀ Take your child with you for antenatal check-ups and let her listen to the baby's heartbeat and (in the later stages) 'help' the midwife or obstetrician feel the baby's position.

'Rhett was easy to prepare for a baby. As a midwife, I did most of my own antenatal care, so he heard the baby's heart on the doppler or on the stethoscope. He loved hearing the sounds of her heart beating, though it was a rare opportunity because I am mindful of the harmful effects of ultrasound. He'd also put his head on my growing belly, kiss her and feel her kick. Because he was breastfeeding, I explained that he'd have to share Mummy's booboos with the baby. I said that babies need lots of attention and Mummy would hold the baby in his old sling. He absorbed it all so easily. We watched some birth DVDs together to prepare him for being at the birth. He was fascinated by it all.

'We still talk about how Kaede was born six months later. And he has a teddy bear and carries it in a sling and breast-feeds it, just like Mummy!'

Rachael

Talking about birth

Whether your child is present at a sibling's birth, is close by to greet the newborn, or visits several hours later, is a choice that depends on your own and your child's needs. But regardless of what you choose, how you talk to your children about birth can leave lasting impressions – you can convey wonder at the power of your amazing body or you can conjure up unnecessary fears.

Toddler tactic: arrange a special friend

If you are having your toddler present at the birth of your new baby, organise to have a support person especially for your child. Then, if she needs to be amused or perhaps taken out (you may change your mind about wanting her around or your toddler may become restless), you can focus on birthing your baby, knowing your child is in good hands.

'All of my children were at each other's birth, and as I birthed four children in five years they were very close together. The transition period with a new baby was easy for the children because I birthed at home and the midwife had become a dear friend, having spent a lot of time in our lives for four consecutive years. Pregnancy, birth and breastfeeding were

normal events in our home and the children's involvement in their sibling's births was, I believe, one of the biggest factors in counteracting sibling rivalry.'

Jo

It depends on the age of your little one how much you explain about birth and how much you involve them. I explained to my own children how my vagina would stretch like a skivvy for the baby to come out and they were fascinated by discussions about the role of the placenta and umbilical cord – and belly buttons! There are some lovely children's picture books that can help you initiate discussion about the birth process. By observing your children at play, talking openly and honestly at your child's level of understanding, you will be able to prepare them for the arrival of a new baby. However, despite your best intentions to involve or explain, toddlers often have their own take on the birth process.

'I gave birth to each of my children in a blow-up pool and I have videos of their births. My three daughters were born with me in a semi-reclining position, for my son I was on all fours. My son, Riley, after watching the births on video, asked why girls come out of vaginas and boys come out of bums. I couldn't understand why he thought that until I realised how

*the positions I was in looked from his perspective. Then it
made sense!'*

Jo

'We planned a home birth for our fourth child. Our older children were twelve, eight and two when little Jaida was born.
During labour, I stripped off and hopped into the blow-up pool
we had set up in the lounge room. My two-year-old daughter Lucy looked at me, then disappeared into her bedroom.
She emerged a moment later completely nude and hopped
into the pool. As I laboured, my husband poured warm water
over my back and Lucy swam around me, patting my leg every
now and then as I moaned. My twelve-year-old son videoed the
birth and my eight-year-old son held my hand as I pushed. Dad
caught the baby!

'Lucy still talks about when Jaida was born, and describes
how her brothers cut Jaida's long tail (the umbilical cord).'

Rachele

The baby arrives

Imagine that your partner has just brought home a new
lover and announced that you are all going to live together. It
will be fun! You will be best friends! After hearing that your

partner loves you and his new lover equally, you are asked to share all your things with this intruder. It also turns out that you won't be getting as much attention as you used to because the new lover is a bit upset about something. Anyway, you are such a clever person, you can do lots of things by yourself now. Oh, and by the way, you must be gentle with the new lover! Wouldn't go down too well, would it?

In *The Emotional Life of the Toddler*, Alicia Leiberman paints a vivid picture of the practical ways a toddler experiences the arrival of a new sibling: 'He now needs to wait more often and longer than ever before for things he needs or wants. He spends more time alone. He is scolded or corrected more frequently as parents try to teach him what he can and cannot do with the baby. Some favourite activities often have to be curtailed because of the baby's needs.'

Is it any wonder your firstborn reacts with shock, and perhaps even a bit of regressive behaviour, when he realises that you are also Mummy and Daddy to the newborn, and that she is here to stay?

'I thought I had done such a great job of preparing my two-and-a-half-year-old Cameron for our new baby. (After reading copious books I understood the significance of using the word "our" in reference to the baby.) Everything was sweet for about

two weeks of breastfeeding "our" new baby but then I think it "clicked" with Cameron that she was here to stay. I don't think I will ever forget him standing squarely in front of me while I was nursing "our" new baby! I remember the look on his face, the tell-tale signs of wanting the "same", the change in body language and the deliberate, yet innocent, trickling of piddle in his pants, which he hadn't done for over a year.'

Miriam

'My son and I had a wonderful relationship until his baby sister was born. On my third night in the hospital my son grabbed my bag and put on my shoes and proceeded to walk out the door, saying, "Mummy come"? I left the next day. My son was at daycare and I went to pick him up with Daddy. I went in alone and my husband followed with our daughter. He saw me and screamed, "Mummy!" We hugged and kissed and he was curious about the little bundle Daddy was carrying.

'My son never really took to me for two weeks. Nana was also in the bad books for tending to the little crying, time-wasting intruder. He threw a lot of tantrums and tried to hit the baby for the next three months.

'I dedicate all the time I have to him when she is asleep. I also make sure we have an outing most days for his benefit. When they are both awake and cranky, the one who is crying *the most and has the greater need usually wins. My husband and I tag team nappy changes and cuddle time. My daughter is mainly down on the floor unless she is crying, which allows my toddler to play with me. I have begun a special box, which is filled with toys and books. I pull it out when I need to be with my daughter or when he is very tired and wants all of my time.*

'He now accepts her as a part of the family and when she cries he tries to comfort her. When he wants to play now, he gives her a toy even though she is too little. The first months can be hard but there is acceptance in the end as I am now finding out.'

Sandra

Helping your toddler adjust to a new sibling

Prepare your toddler for the reality of a baby in the house well in advance – visit friends with babies, point out pictures in books and magazines, and discuss how life might change. You may like to give your child a small album of photos taken when she was a baby, and chat about them with her.

Let your child help prepare for the baby by choosing baby clothes together, drawing a picture for the baby, or making a cake to freeze and eat later at a welcome baby party.

If you have a hospital birth, make sure that when your toddler first visits you – and when you arrive home – someone else holds the baby while you give your older child a special hug. Plan his first visit to the hospital for when he is not tired or hungry and have a special gift from the baby to his older sibling (perhaps a baby doll that can be cared for while Mummy is attending to the real baby).

In hospital and at home, let your older child help while you feed, change, wash and hold the baby.

Set up a corner for feeding times, with special things to occupy your toddler: snacks, drinks, storybooks, a scrapbook and crayons, a CD player with your toddler's favourite songs. While you're feeding the baby, tell her (loudly enough to be overheard!) how great it is to have a big brother or sister.

When the baby is contented (or perhaps as you put him to sleep), tell the baby (again within earshot of the sibling) that you and your older child are going to do something special together such as paint a picture, play with playdough or have a swing, but babies are *much* too little for such a fun activity. Then, when you do something special with your older child, focus your attention on them. This is his or her *special* time. Perhaps somebody else (your partner, grandma or friend) could keep an eye on baby to make this possible.

Introduce changes such as moving from a cot to a bed or starting preschool either well before the baby arrives or several months later. A new baby and the ensuing family upheaval is enough adjustment at one time – even for parents!

Be aware that the green-eyed monster can rear his troubled little head at significant points even after you think your child has become accustomed to his new sibling. For instance, your older child may become surprisingly frustrated (and express this very strongly) as the new baby becomes mobile and starts to intrude on his sibling's space. Also, be sure not to give the baby treasured items – favourite blankets, or toys that belong to the older child – without asking first.

Toddler tactic: create a private space

To prevent resentment when your newly mobile baby gets into your older child's things, set up a place where your older child can play undisturbed. You can put your toddler and his blocks, train set or puzzles in a playpen out of reach of the baby or put a gate on your toddler's room and make a special fuss of giving him his own space, so that pesky little baby can't mess up his 'work'.

Regression, fear of abandonment and anger at the new baby are common ways your child may show anxiety about the arrival of a new sibling. It's best not to react or punish. Instead, offer extra doses of love and comfort, and make an effort to notice and encourage your older child's positive behaviour.

It is *not* acceptable to hurt the baby, but if your child voices negative feelings about the baby, show understanding by saying something like, 'It sounds like you're mad at the baby, maybe because he has been crying a lot and needing so much of my time.' Let your toddler talk honestly about his feelings. Resentment expressed verbally is unlikely to become anger expressed in actions towards the baby.

'It has been a struggle for my three-year-old to handle having a baby brother in the house. She has struggled to share the attention and time we had always given fully to her. My strategy has been to focus on the good and remove the bad. So when he is looking at her and giggling, I point it out to her, and I often tell her how much her baby brother loves her. When he cries, we get her to help by asking her to sing to him, which works well to calm him down. She feels like she is helping us, and is chuffed that she can stop him crying.

'When she is tired, and struggling with the division of attention, she can tend to take it out on her brother physically. We have tried to be strict, but have noticed that at those times it really doesn't sink in and will make her go into a frenzy of attack. So now we gently explain that we don't hurt babies, and we would never let anybody hurt her, and then we remove the baby. The situation calms much quicker this way, and she doesn't feel like the one left out for being naughty.'

Linda

'I had a tough time dealing with my two-and-a-half-year-old daughter when her baby brother came along – she was much more challenging than he was. Her behaviour regressed a great deal. She was almost out of nappies but we had to put them on her all the time. She wanted to be changed like the baby and, to my horror, even weed on herself while I was changing her, and laughed. She became very baby-like in her behaviour.

'My husband worked long hours and I had no support, so we made the decision to get a nanny one day a week. Financially it was a stretch, but I needed help. It made a huge difference to have a day where I had extra hands, and my daughter loved it, too. It allowed us to have some one-on-one time which is really important.

'Her world had changed in a big way and we all adapt to change differently, so I believe it's best not to have any expectations and keep loving and encouraging your kids. Tough times will pass, even if it doesn't feel like it at the time!'

Kelly

Chapter twelve
Becoming independent

We all want our little ones to venture into the world with confidence. But before they can stretch their tiny wings, children need a secure base to lift off from and to return to when they feel a little overwhelmed. Although it can be tempting to force your child to be independent by pushing them into new situations or have them minded by different carers (as you justify that it will be good for their social skills), this can have the opposite effect. Toddlers need to form strong attachments with the special people in their lives and develop a sense of trust and security before they feel safe enough to explore new relationships and experiences. And, just like any other aspect of their development, toddlers vary in their readiness to become 'independent', however you like to define this.

'My baby girl, Anna, has just turned one. My husband and I have a home-based business and just lost a wonderful nanny who has been with us since Anna was born. We decided to

try daycare because Anna is so social and loves being around other children. I didn't particularly like the daycare centre that was down the street, but my husband didn't see anything wrong with it, and when we went to visit, Anna loved it!

'When we dropped her off in the morning she seemed so happy and waved goodbye to us and easily went off with the young girl who received her. That was at 10 a.m. I should have trusted my maternal instinct and picked her up at 2 p.m., or not left her at all, but I let my husband talk me into leaving her longer. We got stuck somewhere until 5 p.m.! I finally left extremely abruptly because I couldn't stand the feeling that Anna needed me. It was so instinctual. I said, "I cannot be here any longer! My baby needs me now!" When I got to the centre poor little Anna seemed changed forever. Normally she is confident, cheerful and funny. She seemed dazed and confused. She was totally traumatised, and it was obvious that she had been crying a lot. She was waving goodbye to no-one in particular. At one point she reached out for the carer, who looked frazzled.

'Until today, nothing bad has ever happened to her. She has had a loving nanny who cared for her in our home with us nearby, giving lots of love and attention. She came around to her old self after about two hours with us, but it was such a heavy, sad experience for Anna, her father and me, and I still *feel that I have hurt her badly. The director of the centre said the first three days are always like this. I can't imagine putting Anna through two more days of what she suffered. I feel like I made a big mistake. I would never do anything to intentionally hurt my baby girl but I made her more miserable than I can bear to imagine because I needed to get some work done.'*

Ashley

Small steps backwards

Even completely secure toddlers can take two steps forward and a step or more backwards along the bumpy road to independence. One day your child will happily wave good-bye and on another, she will cling to your legs; she may have been enjoying family meals at the table for weeks, then suddenly want to sit in her highchair and be fed; or, even though she has been sleeping all night long in her own bed, she may start waking and needing a cuddle in the night.

Sometimes the reasons for returning to 'baby' behaviour are obvious. Your little one may be feeling off-colour or there may be some upheaval (daddy's work may involve travel away from home, there is a new baby or you have had visitors staying). At other times there isn't an obvious explanation for regressive behaviour, although a step backwards can often precede a big developmental leap. Whatever the reasons behind this unpredictable progress on the path to being 'big', most 'backward' steps only last a few weeks at most. Allow your child to rest and feel safe again, rather than pushing him away and forcing him to 'be a big person' before he feels ready.

Don't react strongly if your child reverts to 'babyish' behaviour. Respond with, 'Oh, you want to pretend to be a baby and eat in the highchair.' Without a fuss, she will soon become bored and want to eat at the table again. Encourage 'big' behaviour by appealing to the 'grown-up' nature of your toddler. 'I'm so happy to have a big girl who can hold my hand when we walk to the shops.'

Toddler tactic: teach him to 'use his words'

Give your toddler language to express his feelings. 'I miss Daddy when he has to go away to work, do you?' 'Sometimes I feel angry when the baby wakes up.' As he becomes more capable of expressing his feelings in words, he will no longer have to use baby behaviour to get his needs met. Of course, this will depend on his language and cognitive skills as well as your patient modelling, so please don't expect miracles from a toddler. Just because he can talk well and 'use his words', doesn't mean he can contain his feelings yet.

Above all, try to see things from your child's perspective: consider how you feel when your world becomes stressful or you are about to undertake a new project. Wouldn't it be nice to have some extra support, a hand to hold, a hug? Tiny tots who are just stepping out into the world need support and kind words to help them face new challenges with confidence.

Saying goodbye

If you are leaving your toddler with a carer, don't ever sneak away. This will not help your child become independent because he will either discover that you have left and become upset and confused, or if it's only a short separation he may not even know you have left him and so won't learn the valuable lesson that when you go, you always return. When you leave your child be honest and tell her you are leaving her with her carer.

Create 'goodbye' and 'hello' rituals to teach that although you may leave your toddler for short periods, you will return. At first, practise your 'goodbye' ritual as you leave the room and let her play by herself for short periods.

Help your little one get used to separations gradually. Begin by waving goodbye as your child goes out with another familiar person such as Grandma or a friend for a short walk – often toddlers are happy to leave you, rather than be left.

If you are planning to start your child in any sort of childcare, stay with her at first so she gets used to the environment and feels comfortable with the carers, then leave for short periods – say, an hour at a time – and gradually build up the length of separations. Ask the carers what the daily routine is and introduce this routine at home so that it won't be too much of a shock when you leave your little one. Of course, if you are hiring a carer to be in your own home, your child's patterns should remain the same, so you will need to familiarise the carer with your child's preferred routines and rituals.

Play dates

You need a cuppa with a friend who has a child a similar age to yours, so why not organise a play date for yourselves and your children? Either visit each other's home or meet on neutral territory such as a park. As well as enjoying a bit of company with somebody your own size, you can gently introduce your toddler to the finer points of sharing and socialising. It can be less threatening to a toddler to play with one or two other little ones than to manage the intricacies of playing within a larger group of children who are all beginners at getting along together. And by having parents present, your child can be guided to learn how to 'play nicely'.

Play dates can represent toddler togetherness at both its best and worst: when you put a couple of toddlers together, you can't expect to simply sit back and sip coffee without at least a few 'push and shoves' in between the idyllic moments of cooperative play. To help encourage a positive experience at your toddler's next play date, keep the following helpful hints in mind:

❀ **Timing matters.** A short play date once or twice a week will be enough for a toddler. If he is rushed from one play date to another almost every day, your little one may begin to feel that play dates are more like work than play. It is also important to schedule play dates for a time of day when your toddler is normally rested, fed and in a happy mood, to increase the chances of everyone having fun.

❀ **Keep it short.** Most young toddlers won't be able to manage a long play date. At first, try to limit play dates to about an hour and see how your little one copes. If you stretch toddlers too far too quickly, even with playmates they love, the fun won't last.

❀ **Be realistic.** Remember that one- and two-year-olds tend to play alongside each other rather than engage in games together, and two- to three-year-olds will have trouble sharing and taking turns, so you will need to offer lots of help and supervision to encourage harmonious play.

❀ **Three is a crowd.** When you are starting to organise play dates, invite one little friend at a time, at least until your toddler can happily manage to play and share with other children.

❀ **Offer food.** Just as you and your friend will enjoy a cuppa, your tots can connect over a healthy snack – it will take the edge off potential crankiness, and kids often eat better when they have a little friend to dine with.

❀ **Put away favourite toys.** You can avoid at least some of the squabbles over toys by putting away precious things that your toddler might have difficulty sharing. Instead, set out a few toys that are 'neutral' such as blocks or puzzles and toys that you have two of the same. If your toddler gets cranky about sharing, try a distraction and reassure him that his friend won't take any of the toys home with him. For more about choosing toys for toddlers, see page 128.

❀ **Organise activities.** You don't have to set up your home like a mini-kindergarten every time you have a play date, but it helps to have a few fun activities ready for tiny tots with short attention spans – bubbles and balloons are always winners! (See 'Sensory play' on page 134.)

❀ **Keep a close eye out.** It is important to closely supervise little ones playing together. A child in a new environment is likely to discover potential hazards that your own child may not even be interested in. Also, you will be able to divert disputes before they become fisticuffs!

Playgroup

Places to go, things to do and people to see are all basic needs – for mums! Even if your child would be equally happy with a few empty cartons and dress-up clothes or some sand and water in their own backyard, you are likely to feel deprived of stimulation, company and fun if you don't venture out. Thankfully, you can have just as much fun as your little one by joining a playgroup. There's nothing like mixing with other mums and their little munchkins to help you get things into perspective. Best of all, you can justify this because it's aiding your child's development. So is playing in the backyard, but let's not split hairs.

Playgroup will give your child the opportunity to:

❀ play with and amongst other children
❀ develop a sense of sharing and cooperation
❀ share new experiences
❀ respond to other grown-ups
❀ learn simple rules and routines.

Different playgroups will suit different families – you can join an existing playgroup or you can get together with some like-minded parents and create your own. Contact the Playgroup Association in your state for details about how to start a playgroup (www.playgroupaustralia.com.au).

Toddler classes

Fun and learning go hand in hand at most organised children's activities, and if you join a class with your child you could even take this opportunity to learn a new skill yourself. You could try rollerskating, swimming, dance, music or yoga, all for the sake of optimum child development, of course – a child learns best by imitation! If you feel a bit self-conscious about leaping round, singing in public or (oh dear!) baring your mummy tummy, take heart – you won't embarrass your toddler if you sing out of tune, most of the other mums will be wearing t-shirts over their bathers and the dads in the swim class aren't there to check you out anyway!

Many classes – such as swimming, yoga or baby gym – can be started before your child even becomes a toddler but good toddler classes are age appropriate so don't feel you have missed the boat if you didn't start until now. Some classes can't actually be started before your child is a toddler: your child needs to be able to balance on his feet before he can dance, for instance.

'We go to a lovely tiny tots rollerskating class each week. We started when Sarah was eighteen months old and she loves doing action songs like the birdie dance and the hokey pokey. It's amazing how much fun she has as she is developing coordination, rhythm and balance, not to mention confidence!'

Polly

Some children's activity classes also include parent education as part of the instruction process. You might come home with a stack of creative ideas, games to play or new songs to stimulate your child's imagination for another week.

Although attending a class with your tot can give you special time together, as well as an opportunity to meet other parents, it is best to strive for a balance between providing opportunities and feeling pressured. Children need time to 'just be' as well as to create and explore. Experiences such as a ride on a train or a visit to a farm are also valuable for learning, and your little one (and you) can benefit just as much from a romp in the park as spending hours strapped into a car seat as you battle traffic to deliver him on time to one more educational activity.

Childcare

Sooner or later you will be looking for a trustworthy person to help take care of your child. You can count yourself lucky if you have a doting grandparent or several to look after your tot but many parents don't have such an easy option. Whether you are returning to paid work or need somebody to care for your child while you get your hair and nails done, you will want peace of mind that your child is being cared for by a warm, loving, reliable person.

Childcare falls into four main types: long daycare, which may be provided by a commercially run business, your local council or workplace, or it may be community based such as a kindergarten that offers a long day program; family daycare run by a mother in her own home; occasional care in a creche which may be provided by a commercial centre or a local council; and private carers such as nannies and babysitters. Each one has its advantages and drawbacks, depending on your family's needs. Before checking out childcare options, think about how much you can afford to pay, what you are looking for in a 'you' substitute (do you want one-on-one care, small group care or large but well-supervised groups?), how many days a week you want and the hours you need.

Check what routines and settling techniques are practised by any carer when you are planning to leave your child. For instance, if you have a child who doesn't have the same sleep routine as the childcare facility (such as a daytime nap), ask if they will offer an alternative for a little one who is awake? Sometimes it is possible to manage a happy medium by gradually getting your child used to elements of the carer or centre's routine before leaving her so it isn't a complete shock. If there is a chasm between your mothering style and the carer's approach, weigh things up very carefully before leaving your child – why undo all your own good work by confusing your child now.

With any form of childcare, your child's wellbeing is

paramount so, without becoming too paranoid, do check-up on your carers: if you have a nanny in your home, pop back without warning occasionally or ask a friend to drop by. If your child is in a centre, enlist a friend to snoop on your behalf – she can drop into the centre (making sure your tot doesn't see her if she's well known to them) and request a visit under the pretence that she is considering leaving her child there. You could also 'get off early' sporadically.

Toddler tactic: sleep time at creche

If your child is used to being 'mothered' to sleep, you could help her settle when she is in childcare by leaving a soft toy that has been tucked into your own clothing or a worn t-shirt (so it smells like you) that your toddler can cuddle at sleep times.

Babysitters and nannies

If you choose any sort of private in-home childcare, such as a babysitter or nanny, it goes without saying that there will be a fair bit of groundwork before you find Mary Poppins. You may be lucky and wind up with a gem who adores your child and can also turn her hand to a curry, type a quick letter, clean the house, help with a bit of ironing and keep everybody smiling with her wicked sense of humour. Or, you could be like most of us and have to kiss a lot of frogs!

To find the help you're hoping for:

❀ Ask friends, neighbours and other parents if they know anybody they could recommend. You need to feel comfortable about any stranger you bring into your home to care for the people you love the most.

❀ Before arranging an interview, try to work out whether the person is really interested and suitable. If you go through an agency they do the groundwork and should also conduct police checks. Describe exactly what you want: the locality, working hours, pay and anything else you think is important, from your parenting philosophy to any special needs such as your child's allergies.

❀ Check references thoroughly! Contact the referees and ask how old their children were when this person cared for them, how long they cared for the children, how they related to the children and why they left (if they no longer work with the family). Also ask if they have anything negative to tell you, and if they would employ her again.

✿ Ask about the sitter's experience and qualifications in childcare, and ask for verification. Also ask what training she has in first aid and CPR, and discuss what she may do in emergency situations. A competent sitter will be able to answer these questions and prove they can react confidently and calmly to a crisis. Also try to tick the boxes on the following checklist of qualities: maturity (although a teenager may be perfectly capable of caring for your toddler, it is far too much responsibility for a young person to deal with choking or falls without having an adult present); good judgment; common sense; a friendly personality (do her eyes light up when she talks about her previous childcare experiences?); and a sense of responsibility. Check if she is a smoker (ask and smell), and if she's healthy (she needs to be able to keep up with your active tot!), neat (are her shoes and nails clean?) and organised (ask her how she would organise a typical day?).

✿ When you find someone you like, spend time with them in your house with your child. Watch to see if she seems comfortable in your home, and relates well to your child, and vice-versa. Your goal is to build a relationship with this person and you want to get a good idea of how she interacts with your child before you leave her in charge. You also need to see if the babysitter is respectful of your parenting style. Ask what she would do if your child bit, pushed another child, refused to go to sleep or to eat, cries for you, and so on. If you don't like her response, don't leave her in charge of your child. Above all, go with your gut feelings – do you trust this person with your child?

❀ Maybe your ideal carer is a 'cream of the crop' nanny, if only you could afford her? Consider nanny sharing – essentially, two mums who get on really well, with similar parenting styles, living reasonably close, share the cost of their very own Mary Poppins. Usually one home is the base, or this could be alternated as it suits. This option needs to be carefully worked out with clear ground rules (right down to whether sweets are allowed or not), and communication methods sorted before you engage your nanny. Above all, remember that even the very best nanny isn't superhuman, so be realistic in your expectations, including the ages and number of children you want her to care for.

Family daycare

Family daycare is a flexible set-up where an accredited person provides care for a small number of children (no more than five to seven children, including the carer's own children) in her own home. All carers have to meet standards set by family daycare schemes which are generally supervised by your local council. This is a great option for parents who work unusual hours or want some time out on a regular basis. Because of the small number of children, this is often a good choice for younger toddlers.

'For us, family daycare was a godsend. Without any of my family in Melbourne, I had very little support. When Jessica turned one I tried occasional care for three hours once a week just so I could have a break and do the shopping, but I think she was too young. She seemed to get lost in the large group of kids and was constantly distressed, so I took her out. The private daycare centres I looked at were very big with lots of children and I felt Jessica would never get the care she needed.

'I decided to try family daycare and was placed with a wonderful woman who looked after Jessica for nearly two years, and then I was given a place with another fantastic carer who Jessica just adores. I feel as if she has become part of our extended family, and it is wonderful to have people close by who you trust totally to care for your children. I really like the home environment, the small number of children and the personal relationship the family establishes with the carer.'

Tania

Long daycare

When choosing a centre for your child, always trust your first instinct. You can ask all the people in the world what they think of childcare and which place they recommend, but at the end of the day it's you leaving your precious child, not them! Childcare director Tamika Hicks suggests you ask the following questions when looking for a child-care centre for your child:

✿ How many children are in each age group? It's always good to see smaller-sized rooms since the children don't get as lost as they would in a big space. Look at the age groups, and ask who your toddler will be with. The confident walkers should be separate from the rollers and crawlers.

✿ What do the children eat here? Is it healthy? Does the centre participate in the Start Right Eat Right program, which ensures that the menu reaches 50 per cent of the recommended dietary intake for children (with the remaining 50 per cent being breakfast and dinner at home).

✿ Does the centre have an impressive accreditation certificate (that is, is it all above good to high quality)? If not, ask why.

❀ Are the carers qualified? It is good for assistants to have a TAFE Certificate 3 and group leaders to have a Diploma of Children's Services. Ask if the carers have any additional training or experience. And check on the director of the centre's level of experience.

❀ Are professional development opportunities offered to staff throughout the year?

❀ Is there an orientation process and is it flexible? Does it allow for you and your child to spend time together at the centre?

❀ What is the centre's philosophy? (This should be included in their literature and is a must-read.) If it is not in line with your own philosophy, your answer to whether this is the right place for you is made.

❀ Don't be afraid to ask as many other questions as you need to!

'My little boy has been going to daycare for three weeks, two days a week. I started out leaving him just an hour, and have been slowly building up so that he's now there for a total of six hours a week, including naps. The childcare workers are really loving, and I'm feeling much better about my impending return to work. It hasn't been without difficult moments – I drove away crying one day, after seeing my darling through the

fence looking a little lost in the arms of the childcare worker. He'll have a little cry when I return (in the sense of, 'Oh, yes, I knew there was something missing!'), but the investment in time to slowly build up his confidence has definitely paid off. Time spent hanging around centres to choose the one with the best feel has also paid off.'

Emma

'My twelve-month-old daughter is in daycare Tuesdays and Fridays. We slowly introduced her at eight months of age while I was still on maternity leave, going in one day a week and gradually increasing the hours over a couple of months. It did cost us financially but we didn't have the stress of my first week back at work being her first week in daycare – she already knew the carers and was familiar with the centre.

'I now work three days a week. She is in daycare two days, with her grandparents one day, and with me and her father the other days. We believe this is a great balance.'

Sophie

Chapter thirteen
Love, laugh, enjoy

Time which passes swiftly by, won't stop to hear us though we cry, for days long gone and smiles missed, and damp curls that we should have kissed.

These words were inspired by my 'bonus baby' as I realised how quickly the years had passed since my older children were small and full of wonder.

Go on, get down to your toddler's level and look into her eyes. See the innocence, hear her laughter and feel her joy as you look at the world the way your child sees it. This period of her life is so short, and so special. Make the time to:

❀ Hold your toddler's hand and walk beside him, slowly. Take off your shoes and his and, together, feel the sensations of sand and grass, mud and puddles as you both wiggle your toes.

❀ Take time to watch (without directing him) how he

works at play, and how he is in awe of the smallest things from a line of ants to raindrops dribbling down a window pane or washing fluttering in the breeze. See how excited he becomes at the big things in his world, from Daddy (who is probably the absolute biggest thing in his world!) to the rubbish truck, a digger breaking up asphalt on a footpath, or a plane flying overhead.

❀ Listen carefully to your toddler. Show her she is important and that you value her conversations by looking into her eyes with expression as she chatters to you. Be truly present when she tells you in her own way how much she loves you.

❀ Laugh with your child, especially when he has 'adventures' (or some days you may cry!).

❀ Enjoy every precious moment with your unique, wonderful, amazing little dynamo. Shed your inhibitions, let out the child within and make the most of swinging in the park, jumping in puddles, playing hide and seek, singing out loud in public, wearing jewellery made from noodles and string, and sharing big squishy kisses. All too soon this will pass. You will never get this moment, this hour or this magic year back ever again. So take your toddler in your arms, look into her beautiful eyes and tell her, 'I love you, just the way you are!'

Resources

Allergies and Food Intolerance

Allergy Free

Information and support for allergy-free households; personal and baby products available on-line.

Website: www.allergyfree.com.au

Food Intolerance Network of Australia (FINA)

This site is hosted by Sue Dengate, the author of books on allergies and food intolerance, including *Fed Up* and *The Failsafe Cookbook*. It has a wealth of information and resources including a list of food additives, articles, parenting stories, links and a free newsletter.

Website: www.fedupwithfoodadditives.info

Autism, ADD and Other Disorders

Australian Advisory Board on Autism Spectrum Disorders
The national peak body representing people with autistic spectrum disorders, their families, carers and helpers. Links to autism support organisations in Australia.

Website: http://autismaus.com.au/aca/

Relationships Australia
The Relationships Australia website includes specific ADD/ADHD links, research and support.

Website: www.relationships.com.au/resources/links/add-adhd-specific-links

Breastfeeding

Australian Breastfeeding Association
PO Box 4000
Glen Iris VIC 3145
National Headquarters
1818–1822 Malvern Road
East Malvern VIC 3145
Phone: (03) 9885 0855
Fax: (03) 9885 0866
Website: www.breastfeeding.asn.au

Parenting information and support

Ask Dr Sears
The site of paediatrician William Sears and his sons – also paediatricians. A very informative site offering evidence-based information about all aspects of parenting.

Website: www.askdrsears.com

Attachment Parenting International
Educational materials, research information plus consult-ative, referral and speaker services to promote parenting practices that create strong, healthy emotional bonds between children and their parents.

Website: www.attachmentparenting.org

Baby signing
The site of signing teacher Jo Kennedy. Includes teaching resources, DVDs and workshops.

Website: www.fingersandthumbs.com.au

Child Accident Prevention – Kidsafe Australia
Website: www.kidsafe.com.au

Child and Youth Health South Australia

A wealth of information about parenting and child development.

Website: www.cyh.sa.gov.au

Department of Community Services NSW

Information and links to parenting resources.

Website: www.community.nsw.gov.au/DOCS/
STANDARD/PC_100217.htm

Lifeline

Australia-wide phone/fax: 131 114

National Association for Prevention of Child Abuse and Neglect (NAPCAN)

A large range of information about parenting issues, in leaflet form and on the website.

Phone: (02) 9211 0224

Website: www.napcan.org.au

Natural child

Run by Canadian psychologist Jan Hunt, this site has a collection of articles on various parenting issues, including gentle discipline.

Website: www.naturalchild.org/home

Parenting Research Centre (Formerly Victorian Parenting Centre)

Parenting information and resources.

Website: www.parentingrc.org.au/vp

Parentline

Most states offer a similar service, including information, advice and referrals.

ACT: 13 20 55

NSW: 13 20 55

QLD & NT: 1300 30 1300

SA: 1300 364 100

TAS: 1800 808 178

VIC: 13 22 89

WA: 1800 654 432 or (08) 9272 1466

Pinky McKay

Yes, this is my website! It has informative articles, comprehensive links to local and international health and nurturing sites, and a discussion forum.

Website: www.pinkymckay.com.au

Playgroup Association

Website: www.playgroupaustralia.com.au

Raising Children Network

This website, supported by the Australian Government, includes a wide range of information about child health, development and behaviour.

Website: http://raisingchildren.net.au

World Health Organization

Up-to-date information about child health.

Website: www.who.int

Poisoning

Poisons Information Centre

National 24-hour poisons information.

Phone: 13 11 26

Relationship services

Relationships Australia

Phone: 1300 364 277

Website: www.relationships.com.au

New Zealand Resources

La Leche League New Zealand
PO Box 50–780
Porirua 5240
Phone/Fax: (04) 471 0690
Email: admin@lalecheleague.org.nz
Website: www.lalecheleague.org.nz

Parent to Parent
A support organisation for parents of children with special
needs.
PO Box 234
Waikato Mail Centre
Vialou House
6 Vialou Street
Hamilton 3240
Phone: 0508 236 236, (07) 834 1108 or (07) 834 1153
Fax: (07) 834 1108
Email: p2pnational@compuserve.com
Website: www.parent2parent.org.nz

Parenting with Confidence
Level 2
300 Great South Road
Greenlane Auckland 1005
PO Box 37–708
Parnell Auckland 1001
Phone: (09) 524 0025
Fax: (09) 524 0029
Email: pwc@parenting.org.nz
Website: www.parenting.org.nz

Parentline
(Christchurch)
Phone: (03) 381 1040

Parents Centre
Childbirth and parent education and support, including playgroups and the magazine *Kiwi Parent*.
PO Box 17–351
Wellington
Phone: (04) 476 6950
Fax: (04) 476 6949.
Website: www.parentscentre.org.nz

Relationship Services
Phone: 0800 735 283
Email: receptn@relate.org.nz
Website: www.relate.org.nz

Royal New Zealand Plunket Society
PO Box 5474
Wellington 6145
Phone: 0800 933 922 (24-hours) or (04) 471 0177
Fax: (04) 471 0190
Email: plunket@plunket.org.nz
Website: www.plunket.org.nz

Further reading

Australian Breastfeeding Association, *Your Toddler and Your New Baby*, Melbourne, revised edition 2007.

Biddulph, S. and S., *Love, Laughter and Parenting in the Years from Birth to Six*, Dorling Kindersley Publishers, Melbourne, 2001.

Bumgarner, N., *Mothering Your Nursing Toddler*, La Leche League, Illinois, revised edition 2000.

Crowe, R., and Connell, G., *Moving to Learn*, The Caxton Press, Christchurch, 2003.

Darian, S., *Seven Times the Sun: Guiding Your Child Through the Rhythms of the Day*, Gilead Press, Brookfield, 1994.

Dengate, S., *Fed Up*, Random House, Sydney, 1998.

Einon, D., *Creative Play for 2–5s*, Hamlyn, London, 2005.

Fox, M., *Reading Magic*, Penguin Books, Melbourne, 2001.

Garth, M., *Moonbeam: A book of Meditations for Children*, Harper Collins, Melbourne, 1997.

Grille, R., *Parenting for a Peaceful World*, Longueville Media, Sydney, 2005.

Hunt, J., *The Natural Child: Parenting from the Heart*, New Society Publishers, Canada, 2001.

McKay, P., *Sleeping Like a Baby: Simple Sleep Solutions for Infants and Toddlers*, Penguin Books, Melbourne, 2006.

Masi, W., *Toddler Play*, New Holland, Sydney, 2001.

O'Connell, J., Cummings, R., and Ralston, G., *Eat Right, Don't Fight*, Doubleday, Sydney, 2003.

Solter, A., *Tears and Tantrums*, Shining Star Press, Goleta, California, 1998.

Sunderland, M., *The Science of Parenting*, DK, London, 2006.

Acknowledgements

This book has been such fun to write as its development has paralleled that of my first grandchild, Griffin, as he has entered the toddler 'hood'. It is a privilege to watch this magical stage unfold up close and personal and yet not to be ultimately responsible – to love, laugh and enjoy, knowing that he has fabulous parents who will guide him safely through his many adventures. I am also fortunate to have the very best agent, Jacinta Dimase, and editors, Kirsten Abbott, Miriam Cannell and Kirsten Alexander – all mothers of terrific toddlers. Your support and discussion has been invaluable to the writing of *Toddler Tactics* – thank you!

I would also like to thank every parent who shared their lovely stories about living and laughing with toddlers. I am sorry that some stories have not been included – editorial decisions are not easy but we would have ended up with an encyclopaedia thanks to your amazing enthusiasm for sharing the wonders of your little ones. Without exception,

I am in awe at how creative and patient you all are as you teach and learn from your children every day and I sincerely appreciate that you managed to find time in your busy days to respond to my calls for stories.

Thanks, too, to the groups and individuals who 'spread the word' as I asked questions about how real parents handled the day to day reality of coping with toddlers – from the diverse range of mums' groups and parents who have shared so much at my toddler workshops to the Australian Breastfeeding Association, the Ozmidwifery email list, Melinda Whyman from Natural Parenting Melbourne, Kelly Zantey, director of BellyBelly, Janet Fraser from Joyous Birth, Jo Kennedy, creator and director of Fingers and Thumbs signing classes, early childhood teacher Merrin Bradbury-Butler, awesome mums Donna Shepherd Wright, Tania Delahoy, Jo Hunter, Barb Glare and Yvette O'Dowd, the mums at East Bentleigh Steiner Playgroup and playgroup leader Fran Parshen, whose gentle wisdom and insight has been an inspiration.

I would also like to acknowledge those who have influenced me over the years. Margaret Sasse, founder of GymbaROO, increased my awareness of the links between physical and neurological development and how these affect future learning. The New Zealand Play Centre

Association and La Leche League NZ set me on the road to learning about my own toddlers' development and helping me to fill my parenting toolbox with gentle strategies so I could direct my children's amazing energy without (too many) struggles. And of course, my own terrific toddlers whose boundless energy and enthusiasm have become virtues now that they are young adults.

Index

afternoon tea 162
age gap between siblings 27
aggression 94–100, 131–2
Alfano, Dr Kathleen 131
allergies 191–4, 298
    and sleep problems 243–5
    see also food intolerances
another baby 260–1
    adjusting to 269–74
    bringing baby home 266–9
    preparing toddler for 261–3
    talking about birth 264–6
answering questions 22
artworks 141–4
Asperger's 106
attention deficit disorder 106,
    299
attention span 74

babysitters 288–91
bad dreams 241–2
bad habits 102–7
balance 5, 50, 51, 56–7

bare feet 51
bathtime 163, 226–8
    as bedtime routine 249–50
    drinking bathwater 102–3,
        105
    toys 129
bedroom of their own 255–7
bedtime 163, 164
    bottle 223–4
    delaying tactics 237–8
    relaxation 238–9, 249–55
    routine 238, 246–7, 249–55
    snacks 246
behaviour
    aggression 94–100, 131–2
    bad habits 102–7
    clear instructions 79–80
    and development stage
        74–7
    good behaviour 72–8
    and junk food 87
    setting limits 78–83
    sharing 76, 93–4

tears and tantrums 75–6,
83–93
too-good child 85
biting 95, 96, 98–100
bladder control 210–11
books 129
bottle feeding 195
bowel control 210–11
breastfeeding 194–202, 299
breast-milk 195, 197
bribes 67–70

car seat 17
chewing 185
childcare 286–7
family daycare 291–2
long daycare 293–4
routines 163–4, 287
saying goodbye 279–80
sleep time 288
toilets 217
choices, limiting 81–2
classes for toddlers 284–6
climbing 54–5
clinginess 14
clothing choices 87–8, 98
cola drinks 87, 244
cot to bed 256
cradle cap 229
crawling 7, 8, 49–50
'cross-patterning' 49, 50, 54

crying 75
crying it out 231–2

daily rhythm 159–64
dancing 55–6
daytime sleep 233, 288
defiance 10–11, 13
delaying tactics (bedtime)
237, 238
Dengate, Sue 193
dentist visits 225–6
Dettwyler, Katherine 196–7
dexterity 15
discipline strategies 61–72
diversions 81, 103–4
dressing themselves 20
dressing up 30, 31, 126, 133
dummies 223

eating safely 184–6
eating together 164
emotional intelligence 91–2,
110
emotional promiscuity 76
exploring 144–8
eye contact 44–5

family daycare 291–2
family rituals 169–71
feeding themselves 179–80
finger foods 179

finger paint (home-made) 140
finger-sucking 223
firstborn 26
food
  healthy eating 177–81, 245–6
  preparation 181
  snacks 161, 162, 182–4, 246
food additives 193
food intolerances 192–4, 298
  and sleep problems 243–5
formula feeds 194–5
Fox, Mem 149–50
fussy eaters 187–9

gardening 147
gender awareness 29–30
gender differences 29–31
Goldstein, Professor Jeffrey 131, 132
Goleman, Daniel 110
good behaviour
  praising 72, 78
  teaching 72–8

hair-washing 228–9
hand-washing after toilet 219
highchairs 180, 185
hitting other children 96–7, 98–9

'holding on' for toilet 211

independence 14, 20, 88
  readiness for 275–9
intermittent reinforcement 69

jealousy of baby 271–4
jumping 53–4
junk food 87

Kennedy, Jo 44–5
Kuhl, Dr Patricia 46–7

language skills 9, 15, 18, 19, 22, 29, 30
  see also talking
Leach, Dr Penelope 63
listening 87
long daycare 293–4
lunch 161

magic for every day 171–3
massage 136–7
  bedtime routine 249–51
masturbation 102–3, 105
mealtimes 162–3, 164, 175–207
meditation 236, 253–5
middle children 26
mid-morning snack 161

milk 194–6, 243–4
mirroring 71
morning rhythm 165–7
mummy meltdowns 108–15
music box 56, 127–8
musical instruments 40,
    127–8, 129

'naming explosion' 10, 34
nannies 288–91
nappies, end of 16, 20
new foods 179
'nice voice' 36
night waking 243
nightlight 242
night-time feeds 195–6, 205
nose-picking 102–4, 105
nuts 186

'object permanence' 202
one-year-olds
    aggression 95
    bedtime stories for 252
    behaviour 74–5
    growth and development
        8–13
    night waking 231–3
    play 120, 141
    talking 34
    toys for 128–9
overstimulation 74, 99

personality development
    23–32
place in the family 26–7
play
    aggressive 131–2
    cooperative 120–1
    creative 141–4
    imaginative 133–4
    importance 116–19
    parallel 120
    sensory 134–41
    solitary 120
    suggestions 154–6
    toys 122–30
play dates 121, 280–3
play space 123–4
play stations 124
playdough (home-made)
    138–9
playgroups 120, 121, 283–4
poisons information 304
potties 214–21
power struggles 87–8
practising what you preach
    83
praise 70–2, 78
'pre-operational period' 18

questions, handling 22
quiet time 161–2

reading aloud 19, 38–9, 40, 148–50, 234, 238, 252–3
relaxation for sleeping 238–9
restless sleep 244
rewards 67–70
rolling 56–7
rough play 95–6
routines 157–8
  bedtime 238, 246–7, 249–55
  daily rhythm 159–64
  family rituals 169–70
  morning rhythm 165–7
  weekly rhythm 160
rules 80
running 52–3
rushing toddlers 167–9

safe (childproof) space 13
safe eating 184–6
safe play 16–17
self-esteem 69, 70
'self-talk' 37–8
separation
  regression to baby behaviour 256
  saying goodbye 279–80
separation anxiety 66, 75, 231, 232
setting limits 78–83
shampoo 229

sharing 76, 93–4, 282
shoes 51–2
shouting at child 100
sign language 42–6
singing to child 39
sleep
  bad dreams 241–2
  changing from cot to bed 256
  changing sleep times 233
  at daycare 288
  daytime 233
  developmental stages 231–9
  discomfort 240–1
  and food intolerances 243–5
  games before sleep 234
  night waking 243
  restless sleep 244
  wakeful toddler 230–1
  waking early 242–3
  see also bedtime
Sleeping Like a Baby 234
slime (home-made) 139–40
smacking 63–5, 100
snacks
  bedtime 246
  daytime 161, 162, 179, 182–4, 246
songs at bedtime 251–2

spatial awareness 54
speech *see* talking
spinning 56–7
storytime 19, 38–9, 40,
  148–50, 238, 252–3, 234
Sunderland, Dr Margot 66,
  85, 89

table manners 176
talking 7–8
  concerns about 35
  correcting 38
  development stages 34–5
  encouraging 37–42
  good and bad words 41
  grammar skills 34–5
  'naming explosion' 10, 34
  'nice voice' 36
  parroting 11, 35, 41
  second language 34, 46–8
  and signing 42–6
  social language 41
tantrums 75–6, 83–4
  dealing with 89–90, 91–2
  'holding' 89–90
  in public places 88
  reducing 86–93
  triggers 84, 86
tantrum diary 86, 87
teeth
  and bottle-feeding 195

care 222–6
development 185
television 150–2, 242
  monitoring 131–2
three-year-olds
  aggression 95–6
  bedtime stories 253
  behaviour 76–7
  growth and development
    17–22
  night waking 236–9
  play 120–1, 124
  toys 129–30
thumb-sucking 223
'time out' 65–7
toilet training 20, 208–9
  at childcare 217
  'holding on' 211
  potties, using 214–21
  signs of readiness 211–14
  telling you beforehand 209,
    211, 213, 215–16
  toilets 218–19
  washing hands 219
  when visiting 217
  wiping 219
too-good child 85
toothbrush 223, 224
toothpaste 223, 224
toys
  bath 129

choosing 128–30
less is more 122
plastic 124
rotating 122
sharing 76, 77, 93–4, 282
storage 123
violent 131
toy library 122
twins 27, 28
two-year-olds
  aggression 95
  bedtime stories for 252
  behaviour 75–6
  growth and development
    13–17

night waking 234–6
play 120, 142
talking 34–5
tantrums 75–6
toys for 128–9

wakeful toddler 230–1
waking early 242–3
walking 7–8, 9, 50–2
walks 144–5, 162
water safety 228
weaning 196, 201, 202–7, 234
weight gain 189–91

yoga for children 58